# Delivering Promise

# Delivering Promise

## Equity-Driven Educational Change and Innovation in Community and Technical Colleges

XUELI WANG

Harvard Education Press
Cambridge, Massachusetts

Paperback ISBN 9781682538890

Library of Congress Cataloging-in-Publication Data

Names: Wang, Xueli (Educator), author.
Title: Delivering promise : equity-driven educational change and innovation in community and technical colleges / Xueli Wang.
Description: Cambridge, Massachusetts : Harvard Education Press, [2024] | Includes bibliographical references and index.
Identifiers: LCCN 2023056566 | ISBN 9781682538890 (paperback)
Subjects: LCSH: Community colleges—United States. | Technical institutes—United States. | Educational equalization—United States. | Educational change—United States. | Educational innovations—United States.
Classification: LCC LB2328 .W285 2024 | DDC 378.1/5430973—dc23/eng/20240122
LC record available at https://lccn.loc.gov/2023056566

Published by Harvard Education Press,
an imprint of the Harvard Education Publishing Group

Harvard Education Press
8 Story Street
Cambridge, MA 02138

Cover Art: Ciano Design
Cover Design: Ciano Design

The typefaces used in this book are Carrara, Gotham, and Bradley Hand.

*To the community and technical
college educators and supporters
who participated in this study.*

# CONTENTS

# PREFACE

*And we are literally reinventing a college in a matter of days and building systems in a matter of hours.*

—Turina Bakken, provost emerita of Madison College

MARCH 11, 2020, was an ordinary yet extraordinary winter day in Madison, Wisconsin. It was just a few days before the COVID-19 pandemic pushed most postsecondary institutions into shutdown, changing how they would operate forever. On that dreary morning, I met with Turina Bakken, then the provost of our local comprehensive community and technical college, for a long overdue coffee. The warm ambience and stimulating aura of the coffee shop could not veil the fatigue written all over her presence. She had been up all night thinking about what to do with remote teaching and learning in anticipation of the unavoidable pivot to come in just a matter of hours. The decision later that day ended with the college officially closing on March 16, 2020. Over coffee, we talked and exchanged many concerns about the programs for which remote education was hard to imagine, faculty who would have to build skills and expertise quickly in a world in which they were not comfortable, and students who didn't have stable access to technology—not to even mention those who lost their jobs and faced severe food and housing insecurities. As we left the conversation, I said, "Turina, I wish I could do more to help." She responded, "Xueli, I thought about canceling this morning, but I needed this conversation today. We will get through this. We will be better for this. Not sure how, but we will."

Turina is my treasured colleague, friend, and thought partner; a former doctoral advisee who completed an award-winning dissertation on how community college faculty develop and advance as innovative leaders; and a fiercely equity-centered educator. In the days that followed, indeed, Turina and the college team moved mountains, quickly making available laptops and hot spots for students and testing dozens of virtual simulation software for courses that were traditionally in person to identify the most accessible ones. Quoting her in a story from our local newspaper, "instruction, student services, technology services have literally [been] created and built from the ground up—systems that, in the world as we used to know, would have taken weeks, months, even years. And we are literally reinventing a college in a matter of days and building systems in a matter of hours."[1]

I was undeniably and immeasurably proud of her. However, I share this story for reasons far beyond myself, or even Turina. It is the countless exchanges and moments like this with my community and technical college partners that serve as my greatest inspiration and urgency in how, as educational researchers and leaders, we should not only reflect but truly act on everything that we say we care about. Like many of my scholar and practitioner colleagues, I am profoundly moved by what the American community college represents: access, mobility, and a remarkable institution built on the premise of *innovation*. However, my journey as a community college researcher for over a decade was far from linear; it was filled with new learning, unlearning, and relearning, especially in light of the place and role of *equity*.

Indeed, community and technical colleges have grappled with innovation and equity since their inception.[2] Yet these two threads have not been addressed often in close tandem. Innovative practices without equity as a guiding light run the risk of perpetuating inequality; and equity solutions must be approached with innovative ideas that crack the persistent, stubborn equity gaps. Like what happened with Turina, her team, and her college, there could not have been a more precipitating time than the COVID-19 crisis to fuse innovation and equity into one charge. Since the spring of 2020, community and technical colleges across the country have faced unprecedented challenges to their daily operations.[3] They rose to the occasion over and again with the spirit of innovation that runs deep in their tradition. However, if detached from an equity lens, these rapid changes may end up exacerbating already widening gaps in educational access and outcomes among a student population already disproportionately affected by the pandemic, essentially defeating the purpose of innovation and leaving unaddressed the needs of minoritized students.[4]

As I was both motivated and challenged by the influx of new practices, often with hidden or overt tensions around who benefits and who is not well served, I found myself revisiting that March 11, 2020, conversation with Turina as a reminder and inspiration. It practically compelled me to embark on the research project behind this book.[5] The 126 community and technical college educators that I had the privilege to interview, and in some cases visit with, between October 2021 and March 2023 have collectively pushed not only my own thinking but the larger base of knowledge, wisdom, and research evidence of what equity-driven educational innovation means and looks like. Although conceptualized and written during COVID-19, this book is not about the pandemic per se; rather, it depicts how this catalyzing crisis set in motion a series of changes and adaptations that require community and technical colleges to not only do what they are known historically to do—to innovate—but equally important, to confront the equity tension head-on. The colleges were all grappling with massive issues of concern as the pandemic dawdled, particularly in the areas of teaching, learning, and faculty development; student services and support; critical use of data; institutional culture and morale; and partnerships with industry, universities, and local communities. These challenges did not emerge from nowhere—they have been enduring ones predating the pandemic. But they have become that much more difficult and at times they seem nearly impossible to confront and overcome. The reflective experiences and insights of the educators in this book shine a light on how these challenges can be tackled with innovation that centers equity as both a process and an outcome, both in times of dire need and into the far future.

Before I detail these educators' quest for change, it is important for me, as the researcher and author of the book, to disclose what I mean by "equity" and "innovation"—the centerpieces of this work. First and foremost, the imperative for equity in education is deeply rooted in centuries-long systemic barriers that have led to significant disparities and disproportionalities, particularly across racial and socioeconomic lines. These inequities permeate all levels of educational policy and practice, influencing not only the structures and resources but also the mindsets and daily practices of educators. In the context of my research, equity represents an ongoing process aimed at ensuring that underserved and minoritized students, as well as undersupported institutions like community and technical colleges, have the necessary access, experiences, and resources to reach their fullest potential. This involves providing holistic support that honors the unique realities and needs of marginalized groups while actively removing barriers to access at both individual and organizational levels.

Innovation—inextricably linked to change leading to something new, renewed, or different—cannot be disentangled from equity. Innovation in education must be equity-guided and -driven. As a result, innovation transpires when we see two things happen. First, innovative practices disrupt and change our past assumptions, emboldening us to unlearn, undo, dismantle, and rebuild; it is not simply additive or continuous. Second, true innovation must result in transformed experiences for the better among those minoritized groups, especially students, to whom we owe an equity debt.

These personal reckonings gained texture and clarity through my research and writing of this book—one brought to life by a study conducted with, from, and for practitioners who aspire to promote equity, instigate change, and foster innovation in their daily work at community and technical colleges. They are the main drivers that anchor change and innovation within their organizations. Thus, while organizational change isn't my primary focus, it is intricately woven into the experiences and insights of these practitioners who actively work toward positive institutional transformation. Those of you choosing to read this book may have contended with some similar experiences and ideas over the past few years of the pandemic. It is my sincerest hope that this book will serve as a sounding board that puts all your own reflections in conversation with the innovations, tensions, learnings, and unlearnings uncovered in my book to shine a critical light toward a truly equitable community and technical college education.

# INTRODUCTION

## *Propelled to Innovate Through Turbulence and Undercurrents*

"SO, AS I MENTIONED to my students, this pandemic situation was like pushing the fast-forward button for us." Shawn uttered these words as we finally settled into our Zoom interview after adjusting sound, mute, unmute, all those pandemic-introduced virtual nuances—those that always challenge us, no matter how familiar they may have already seemed. Identifying as a Black man, Shawn is a biology instructor and department head at Keystone College, a comprehensive community and technical college in the Midwest[1] where he also serves as a coordinator of the college's STEM Scholars Program—a program aimed at advancing completion and transfer in science, technology, engineering, and mathematics (STEM) fields of study among racially underrepresented students. Long before the pandemic, Shawn and I had corresponded via email a few times to talk about high-impact practices that facilitate transfer, a commitment that we shared.

Shawn was one of my very first interviews. I start this introduction with him not because of that, though; little did I know that fortuitously, what Shawn and I talked about that day would encapsulate the many takeaways from my conversations with the 126 educators I interviewed. Interestingly and figuratively, how he and I navigated our way into the Zoom interview—that feeling of being in constant anticipation of coming up short on resolving what felt like old, familiar problems—captures that frustrating and frustrated state of inertia regarding perennial issues of concern that faced community and technical colleges long before COVID-19.

Such as the high failure rates in college math and other introductory courses.[2] These rates have become even worse during the pandemic in some of the courses Shawn personally taught. But Shawn is no longer willing to accept that as just another hard problem to solve. These courses have had "an extremely high failure rate because we have taught them *the same way for fourteen years*," Shawn emphasized with a tone of deep, reflective earnest. "Maybe we need to rethink how we teach it. Maybe it's not that we need to focus so much on the students, but we need to focus on how we teach it. And we need to teach it differently." Indeed, as I detail in chapter 2, Shawn completely overhauled his teaching approach, not just adapting the existing content for the new pandemic virtual reality, but also exemplifying how rigorous instruction can and should be enriched—rather than diluted—through a human-centered approach that honors the diverse assets and strengths of his students.

Shawn's experiences are some of the foremost tides of the sea change about to come in the sector. Right across the same college, the change started with a seemingly small but difficult move to pause study abroad earlier in 2020. Then, two weeks later, many more "gut-wrenching" decisions were made that affected thirty thousand students. Renee, vice president of academic affairs and faculty development at the college, described these decisions—moving courses online and taking away in-person options—as "gut-wrenching" for a reason: technical education is a vibrant part of the college's offerings that had largely operated in an in-person modality. But the college had to act fast. "And so, thinking back of the speed, where we went from thoughtful consideration of something that impacted a handful of students to making major strategic decisions that impacted every student and every employee, it was really quite something," Renee recalled.

Shawn and Renee were far from alone in feeling this sense of urgency to do business differently. Joining them across thousands of miles is Boricua, vice president and chief student services officer at Afton Community College in the South, who was serving as assistant dean and registrar at the outbreak of the pandemic. His immediate worry was student access—"access to technology, access to internet, access to employees, access to the college," not so much for the small percentage of the students who were OK with remote access and online learning, but rather the students who needed direct contact. It then dawned on him: "Oh my gosh! We have workflows and processes that don't align with what we have going on!" Boricua's strong gut reaction actually reflects a dissonance that he had felt for a while, a dissonance that comes from the duality of access being promised, yet not always delivered. "We are [a] community college. What is our structure, and why is it that we exist the way we do?" This question consistently guided Boricua's thinking. However, it was during the initial moments of the pandemic, when access—a fundamental pillar that provides community colleges with both structure and purpose—was abruptly taken away that Boricua was able to clearly articulate the dissonance. This moment also accelerated the progress he had been making toward fulfilling the commitment of access through the establishment of a student resource center, an innovative initiative I describe in chapter 3.

While every educator I spoke with acknowledged the need for swift action, there was an underlying apprehension about the potential consequences of hurried implementation—a sentiment particularly voiced by Claudia, coordinator for student services at Midwestern State Association of Colleges, who supports the work of student services staff across the state's community and technical colleges. Claudia and her fellow colleagues' primary concern in their roles has always been the most underserved populations: students with disabilities, students of color, veterans, international students, refugees, and immigrants, among others. Different from most of the responses I got when asked about first reactions and thoughts when the pandemic hit, Claudia's was a more measured, introspective one, given after a considerable pause:

> It felt like initially, when COVID-19 came about, I think there were a lot of people who were ready to act, ready to move, and I think that was necessary in a lot of ways. But my concern was action without being informed by the people who may be most impacted, and what are the ways that we can amplify, gather, share the experiences of the students that are most marginalized, so that when we're reacting in these different ways, it can be informed. I would say that was my big concern, and I think part of that was: How are we hearing students [who are least heard]? What avenues can I create to be able to hear them?

While Claudia's response wasn't a typical initial one, nearly all of my participants touched on something similar to her insight later in our conversations. It's the immeasurably difficult-to-solve puzzle of how to instill equity as a guiding light for change and innovation, part and parcel of which transpires throughout the rest of the book.

Shawn, Renee, Boricua, and Claudia, along with many of their contemporaries in this book, view the pandemic not only as an emergent crisis causing massive turbulence that they must respond to, but perhaps more subversively, an accelerator that fast-forwarded them into a quest for permanent solutions to some of the most obstinately pounding issues facing community and technical colleges. Despite the stormy sea change that the pandemic seemed to have triggered, these educators all came to terms with the fact that these are not suddenly new problems owing to COVID-19. Through their informed lens, they recognize the underlying issues that long predated the pandemic—enrollment concerns; how to deliver on the open-access mission with limited and dwindling resources; abysmal passing rates of key gateway courses, which derail students from progressing; low transfer and completion rates; and the list goes on—all against the backdrop of lasting equity concerns about how to level the playing field for the most underrepresented and underserved populations. It is thus imperative that I further unpack these enduring challenges, as they are the real, deep undercurrents that undergird this book.

To address the aforementioned problems, we must constantly recalibrate against the ever-evolving societal and educational landscape that grounds the institutions discussed in this book. Therefore, I must delve into several definitional and contextual issues, the messiness and tensions entrenched within which help position these institutions in both historical and contemporary lights. The first issue to address is how to depict these very institutions.

## DEFINING THE INSTITUTION: GROUNDED IN "COMMUNITY," NUANCING WITH "TECHNICAL"

I developed this book's title to be intentionally inclusive of "community" and "technical." Simple as it may appear, coming up with the most precise term to capture the "two-year" institutions in the United States is a mission nearly impossible. Designed aspirationally to serve multiple societal needs, the institutions began at the turn of the twentieth century as "junior" colleges—an extension from high school to college level while also being a mechanism to maintain the social status of the university, especially the upper-level undergraduate education—to accommodate the increasing number of high school graduates.[3] As these institutions continued to meet the existing and emerging needs of their local communities and grew in public support, many of them eventually took on the name "community college." It is a term that perhaps holds the greatest currency and appeal today in literature and practice. At the same time, the rise of workforce training needs and related legislation to support career and technical education resulted in the naming of some colleges being more reflective of the "technical" and workforce development foci of their mission, such as trade, vocational, or, more contemporarily, technical colleges.[4] In many cases, "community" and "technical" coexist in the colleges' names; in other cases, the institutions primarily use "technical" as their main brand, although many operate much more comprehensively than a "technical" college by providing developmental education, transfer pathways, continuing education, and dual enrollment, among other broader functions.

Ultimately, for this book's title, I landed on the term "community and technical colleges." I was drawn to this framing as it offers a uniquely nuanced view of the multiple and evolving missions and functions of these open-access institutions that primarily offer associate degrees. What is more, while I do personally believe that "community college" is the more encompassing term, the technical education mission does not receive nearly enough distinct attention and treatment in the literature, despite often being an entwined part of these institutions' identity and offerings.[5] Further, this term puts "community" and "technical" on equal footing, given that many participants included in this book work at technical colleges. Although I strive to maintain consistency and nuance in depicting specific colleges throughout this book, ultimately, I personally resonate with the term "community college" most due to the very meaning of, and broad connotations embodied in, the word "community." For these reasons and for simplicity, when engaging more broadly with empirical and policy contexts, I tend toward using "community college."[6]

## DRIVEN BY PRESSURES, INNOVATING WITH LESS

Community colleges have been facing mounting pressures well before the pandemic. According to a 2020 report by the National Center for Education Statistics, enrollment fell by 25 percent between 2010 and 2018 for these institutions.[7] A Community College Research Center report suggests that the pandemic further accelerated these enrollment declines, with a drop of nearly 11 percent between Fall 2019 and Fall 2020—a much sharper downswing compared with a 0.25 percent drop among four-year colleges and universities.[8]

The intensifying enrollment declines are deeply concerning, as community colleges are built on the foundation of access. In the current postsecondary policy arena, which boasts a shift from access to success—largely propelled by national college completion efforts by the Obama administration and organizations such as Complete College America and Achieving the Dream particularly for community colleges—the emphasis on access seems to have fallen a bit off the radar, but it never really left the scene.[9] Indeed, enrollment concerns persistently affected countless community colleges during the college completion era. A poignant case in point: in the state of Wisconsin where I am situated, largely owing to declining enrollment, UW Colleges—the former key transfer feeder and practically the entire community college sector in the UW System—went through a series of painful restructuring measures between 2010 and 2017 that ultimately led to a permanent closure.[10] Similar examples can be found in a few other states, such as the University System of Georgia and the Vermont State College System, where colleges were closed or forced to downsize due to dwindling enrollment.[11]

The threat posed by sluggish enrollment goes viral beyond the issue of access. Alberto, president of West Bank College in the Midwest, was deeply wary of how the dismal enrollment trends exacerbate the already dire scarcity of resources allocated to his college, which in turn affects its ability to hire and retain staff and faculty:

> There are going to be declines if we do nothing. We are down to, like in our non-personnel expenses, to just what we need to turn on the lights and keep the heat going, because, as you know, living here in the Midwest and this part of the world, you gotta keep that heat in the

winter. Primarily because of enrollment declines, but also state appro-
priation is not keeping up with inflation and adjustments for cost of
living. That's in essence what our bargaining units are getting, 2 percent, 3 percent here and there. Obviously, cost of living has gone up
much higher in the last few years, and we are nowhere near making
adjustments of salaries for that.

Even worse, such challenges end up affecting future students in the form
of higher tuition costs, Alberto added. "Half of our tuition is state appro-
priation, and half is student tuition. Last cycle around, the state didn't
give us any money, and we had to raise tuition on students 3.5 percent."

During the pandemic, temporary solutions were offered through
emergency funds to sustain enrollment, but long-term solutions require
forward thinking, which is also challenged by a lack of stable funding,
according to Renee:

> We started thinking about how we could use that funding [emergency
> funds] to jumpstart capacity that would lead us to where we were
> going to have to go in the future after all this. And one of the struggles
> we're having now is we have built all these new high priority needs but
> the grant, the money's gone. Used up. So how do we now continue to
> support our existing faculty and programs, but also now when we're
> in a budget crisis because enrollment's down, how do we continue to
> fund and keep those folks here driving that strategy?

While permanent solutions still seem as elusive as available resources
to sustain these vital institutions and their missions, innovation
remains in the DNA of community and technical colleges, exemplified
by Boricua's words when describing what kept him going amid endless interlacing challenges over the past few years: "For me, it was, how
do we create something different? How do we become visionary? How do
we become innovative, and what do we do with what we have? How
do we transform the work differently to make sure that all students'

needs are met?" Through ideas and actions, trial and error, the community and technical college educators in my book gave their definitions, meanings, and hopes to innovation. While they defined "innovation" in widely diverse ways, they all seem to embrace the concept as an inherent part of what they do, often underlined by a hint of pragmatism.

At first glance, many of the educators described innovation as "trying new things" and having "the agility to respond" in a "proactive" way. Going deeper, though, it is clear that innovation must adapt to students and meet them "where they need to be met," including their learning. It's about "doing better for students," taking a hard look and asking what systems need to be in place or taken away, what needs to be done or not because it creates barriers. These educators also recognized the importance of institutional culture and infrastructure that promote and sustain innovation by fostering collaboration and support for one another to better serve all students, staff, and their institutions. As the rest of the book shows, the collective insights of these educators culminate in a profound understanding of innovation as an adaptive process that meets students where they are, dismantles barriers, and fosters a supportive institutional culture despite shrinking resources.

## EQUITY, PERSISTENT CHALLENGES

While the discussions of innovation often render lots of optimism, my book shows that treating innovation as its own construct alone does not get community and technical colleges where they aspire to be. In particular, complicating the stubborn cycle of problems delineated earlier are unyielding inequities—concerns that have always been present since day one and yet are often misunderstood, conflated, and intentionally or unintentionally shrouded. That's why an in-depth discussion of equity is in order here.

For the great length of the community college history, equity was primarily framed by and conflated with access. For many community college practitioners and researchers alike (my past self included), these institutions' open access is equated to serving the equity agenda, often citing a disproportionately large number of students who wouldn't have had the opportunity to access postsecondary education. Structural reforms tend to be offered as solutions for inequities. These reforms adopt a neutral stance with explicit or implicit assumptions that they are in service to all students. Then, in terms of the mentalities that transpire in practice, a seemingly innocent yet powerful assumption prevails: since we do work on or within community colleges, we of course are doing equity work, something just second nature to us. This assumption is dangerous, though, because it is essentially equity-oblivious, and I want to unpack this a bit more through a personal experience.

In 2019, I participated in a meeting in my capacity as an advisory board member for a project with the goal of boosting transfer in STEM areas of study. The project description referenced equity as a focus. During the half-day meeting, the team talked about new prerequisites and a new competency test to make sure community college transfer students were "ready." But something I was holding my breath for was missing. So finally, I posed the question, "Could you speak about how your project addresses issues of equity in transfer?" It took a while for me to get a somewhat bewildered response: "But we work with community colleges. We work with transfer students. They are the most diverse institutions and students, so of course we are addressing equity!" It was such a familiar response, to which I said:

> I am smiling and nodding because what you said resonated with the past me, especially earlier in my research career, but I've learned and unlearned things about equity that challenged myself to revisit that assumption. I was hoping to hear how your efforts in developing new prerequisites, tests, and partnerships *intentionally* took into consideration questions like: Among the diverse transfer-intending student group, who gets access to these new opportunities and who may not?

For whom will these new opportunities act as additional new structural barriers, *not* because they are not capable or don't work hard enough? And perhaps before anything else, were these new efforts really responding to the needs of transfer-aspiring students, or something else could be done instead to make transfer a more seamless process and experience, especially for those who persistently were left out?

To the colleagues' credit, we have since followed up with multiple thought-provoking conversations, and we continue to grow together to this day.

So the moral of this story is this: well-intended efforts with the unquestioned assumption that equity is inherent can end up being more equity-impeding than anything. This approach is not well aligned with our genuine intent to promote equity—indeed, it practically perpetuates inequity, as we bypass a deliberate process where we must name inequities in their specific, contextualized forms in order to reduce them. And this process often, simply yet sadly, involves eliminating barriers that have been at work for too long at the systemic level—where resources, advantages, and privilege are unequally distributed and thus inequitably accessed, especially based on minoritized identities and backgrounds, notably race and its intersection with income, gender, ability, mental health, age, sexual orientation, first-generation status, citizenship status, international student status, and more.

I hope this context helps ground the long-standing disparities that we see within community colleges—referred to by some as "equity gaps"—that have long been caused by systemic, inequitable education policies and practices, through no fault of students and their families and backgrounds. Enrollment rates among students of color, especially Black, Asian, and Native American students at community colleges were already on a gradual decline since 2012 according to annual data from the National Center for Education Statistics.[12] While the pandemic caused enrollment to drop across postsecondary education, enrollment rates tumbled significantly in community and technical colleges, about 20 percent or more across underrepresented groups including students of color, adult students, and student parents.[13] When it comes to transfer, a 2020 National Student Clearinghouse Research Center report showed that white students were more likely to transfer (53.2 percent) than Hispanic/Latinx or Black students (37.2 percent and 28.4 percent, respectively).[14] Turning to credential completion rates, again, we see a major gap (roughly 15 percent to over 20 percent) between Black and Hispanic/Latinx students and their white and Asian counterparts based on a 2022 National Student Clearinghouse Research Center report following a Fall 2016 cohort of beginning college students.[15]

My participants share these exact same concerns. John, vice president of academic affairs at Pointe College in the West, spoke with blunt honesty to the issue of equity from his range of experience as a long-time educator, researcher, and leader across various community colleges: "It was basically students of color not coming back [enrollment or completion]. So, our identities as a system are going to be again taxed because we are very much paid by, in my state, butts in seats were the typical norm, but also on success and equity types of standards. So, we've got to start taking those things extremely seriously and making sure that the experience is the best for every student that enters our doors because we have fewer of them." John named the issue at the core of inequities— inequity is race centered and is an issue of institutional accountability. He went on about how the system as is simply can't keep operating in the same way: "So, the need to address equity is created. Because of the economic crisis. But it *really* gets you to stop and think about what your purpose is. Why are you here? What is your why? And you'd better be able to explain that to students."

More poignantly, these equity concerns were just a microcosm for what was happening in society writ large. In particular, racial inequities were heightened during the pandemic, coinciding with blatant racial injustices brought to public light by the police killings of George Floyd,

Breonna Taylor, and others. These incidents elevated or sparked larger racial equity movements, including Black Lives Matter, Stop Asian Hate, and other antiracist demonstrations. COVID-19 blew the lid off many long-simmering societal problems—in this case, growing racial tensions that could no longer be avoided. The community and technical colleges in my book are no exception. Institutional statements and speeches from institutional leadership were filled with an explicit focus on race, racism, or racial inequities, often in the wake of the George Floyd murder but also long afterward. Not only did the statements call out these tragedies using terms such as "police brutality," "right-out racism," "injustice," and "racist policies," another somewhat rarely seen theme of these statements and speeches was their emphasis on racism as a larger societal issue that affects everyone and every domain of society. As a telling example, the president of one of the largest community colleges in the Midwest said, "[Police brutality] must end. We simply cannot stand by and say, 'It doesn't affect me.' ... It affects you, even if you don't think it does."

It turns out that these larger societal contexts and movements had formed the perfect storm that compelled college leaders, faculty, and staff to confront equity gaps at their colleges and in their own practices. In many ways, these volatile times offer a unique opportunity to examine how these practitioners grapple with long-existing equity concerns as they reach this historic tipping point, and to reflectively interrogate long-standing structures and practices that shape racial inequities. Neither are these individuals or their efforts perfect; many times they flounder; many other times they question the many things they do or don't do.

Similar to innovation, I intentionally asked my participants how they make meaning of equity. Some of their responses converged at the textbook-version definition of the term due to the sudden surge of diversity, equity, and inclusion (DEI) trainings; others were still evolving or even struggling to make sense of this dense concept. Regardless though, my participants largely demonstrated a change orientation, attentive to developing and growing equity efforts, all the while grappling with how commitments transpire in action. Their willingness to tackle the complexities of equity with tenacity, along with their pragmatic and innovative approaches, is a potent reminder of the transformative impact that can be achieved when genuine commitment and introspection intersect.

## CENTRAL ARGUMENT

Change and innovation are not new themes for community and technical colleges. Indeed, this book heeds the many illuminating insights and progress made by numerous feats of innovation, including those as recent as the Achieving the Dream network, Guided Pathways model, the League for Innovation in the Community College, and the Student Success Center Network.[16] There have also been those more sporadic ones that focus on a particular function like the community college baccalaureate, or a stakeholder group such as faculty.[17] However, change and innovation have not traditionally been studied through an equity lens in ways that center and embed equity throughout rather than as an add-on or afterthought. There is yet to be systematic research that comprehensively documents equity-driven change and innovation catalyzed by the pandemic and interrogates what this means for the future of community and technical college education.

But despite the timing of the pandemic, this book's central message is a message of hope and possibilities; it illuminates the vast potential of community and technical colleges as sites of equity-driven educational innovation. Reconciling the many paradoxes, tensions, challenges, and promises, the central argument is that innovation and equity are the two key ingredients of a just community and technical college education, and one won't work without the other. Despite the best intentions, the most powerful mechanism that has perpetuated inequities is the often invisible, nimble resistance to change and innovation, the default to the status quo.[18] That's why it takes true innovation to crack the stubborn cycle that reinforces inequities. At the same time, what's meant to be innovative is not true innovation if it does not center equity throughout. Historically, innovation has often been detached from an equity lens; rather, it has been approached in an idealistic, isolated vacuum without sufficient care and attention to what, why, and for whom the innovation is meant to address and serve in equitable ways. In other words, we have not paused often enough to ask: Is our innovation leveling the playing field, or is it going to unlevel it further? The pandemic propelled those in community and technical colleges to confront these thorny issues in an accelerated, intense, and honest way. In essence, innovation and equity are inextricably linked, and true innovation can't happen without equity being front and center in the equation.

Coming back to Shawn, as we neared the end of the interview, we chatted about how he would go about adopting innovative ideas and making changes to truly, equitably serve the students he intended to serve. In the interim, he quickly looked up the words "innovation" and "equity" on his phone but decided he didn't like the definitions. What he left me with was a practitioner's most practical yet profoundly incisive approach to enacting equity-driven innovations: "If we introduce something new or innovative, we must look at how that affected students coming right out of high school versus someone who's forty coming back to school. How that affected racially underrepresented minorities? How that affected our first-gen students? We have the ability to do that. We have the analytical tools to do that."

## WHAT'S BEHIND THIS BOOK—A STUDY OF CHANGE AND INNOVATION TO SERVE THE EQUITY AGENDA

With that, Shawn's interview kicked off the qualitative data collection phase—the heart and soul of the larger mixed methods research project that I launched during the height of the pandemic. The overarching goal of the project is to interrogate changes and innovations in community and technical colleges, with a focus on their equity implications for under-represented and underserved populations. I started the initial phase of the project in mid-2020 with a set of quantitative analyses—specifically text mining techniques that integrate machine learning, statistics, and linguistics—to identify patterns and trends within public news sources and media that detailed COVID-19-spurred responses and changes in a Midwestern state. This set of text data analyses allowed me and my research team to harness the massive amounts of information to glean a bigger picture of the initiatives and adaptations cropping up around the institutions in the state, including types, key patterns and priorities, magnitudes, and how they evolved over time. While these data provided a valuable glimpse, I knew these findings were still one piece of the larger story. Qualitative work was sorely needed to not only complement quantitative findings, but more important, to fully unravel the complexities and nuances of the what, how, why, and so-what of this influx of new efforts and initiatives in relation to the enduring and emerging equity concerns described earlier.

I was thus motivated to start conducting qualitative interviews and case studies with various stakeholders to do just that, including faculty, staff, administrators, and executive leaders.[19] I focused on these individuals because their actions, behaviors, and feelings constitute the institutional daily life and closely affect students, thus offering a credible (albeit imperfect) lens into the institutional realities with regard to change, innovation, and equity.[20] I was able to include community and technical college stakeholders from institutions across seven states (three in the Midwest, two in the West, and two in the South). While the vast majority of the research activities occurred in the Midwest, the geographical extension allowed me to explore what was going on beyond the Midwest toward relevant implications across the diverse range of institutions and systems. Many of the insights and examples I outline in this book will hopefully resonate with educators and leaders nationally. Specifically, I draw on interviews, site visits, and volumes of news articles and written documents related to interview participants to illuminate optimal approaches to equity-driven educational change and innovation. For more information on how I conducted the study, the methodological appendix offers much greater detail on research procedures and techniques.

Here is a preview of the rest of the book. Chapter 1 takes a human-centered approach to depict how the educators grapple with innovation and equity in their professional capacity, and equally important, do all this as whole persons, with their own share of challenges. In many cases, their experiences also illuminate some of the thorniest issues in education in dire need of innovation, all complexified by profound equity gaps. In each of the remaining chapters, I deal with a core aspect of community and technical college education; present some of the most compelling issues, challenges, and possibilities for its innovation guided by an equity lens; and offer a set of directions for the future. These discussions are embedded with storytelling of individual interviews and occasionally case studies to lend richer, more holistic contexts. More specifically, chapters 2 and 3 cover teaching, learning, and student support that honors the whole person in compassionate and educationally meaningful ways. Next, chapter 4 engages critical production and use of data as a key precondition for supporting innovative efforts that serve equity goals. Chapter 5 delves into equitable partnerships and community building to facilitate change and innovation. Chapter 6 addresses burnout and highlights the importance of promoting an institutional culture rooted in humanity, kindness, trust, and equity to drive positive change and innovation. Chapter 7 presents findings from an in-depth case study of a science pathway program at a Midwestern technical college. It is a case that encapsulates some of the most innovative mindsets and practices across the key facets covered in the book. Chapter 8 concludes the book and issues a path toward fostering equity-driven educational innovation at community and technical colleges.

At the end of chapters 1 through 8, I include brief questions for reflection geared toward practitioners, policy makers, and researchers.

Throughout the process of doing this research leading up to this very moment wrapping up the book, I have found that often, a transformative journey starts with finding or creating a space that emboldens reflectivity and vulnerability. My participants showed me that the beginning of real change is often marked by recognizing our own vulnerabilities, or just that we are humans who have limits; owning our past mistakes or imperfect practices; and recognizing and doing the work ahead. In that spirit, I pose these reflective questions, in part as continued dialogue with my participants long after our conversations and as a sounding board for the readers of this book engaging in equity-driven work in the policy, practice, and research spaces.

Declining enrollment, stagnant completion of credentials and transfer, and uneven and unequal barriers experienced by minoritized students, all against the ever-increasing pressures of doing more with less, compounded and converged as the world was thrown into the COVID-19 pandemic. It has been an era punctuated by uncertainty and turmoil. It has also been an era that propels community and technical colleges to take a sharp turn in a quest to address their longest-standing challenges with equity-driven change and innovation.

# 1

## Built for the Moment, Sustained by Humanity

*How are we going to continue delivering on our promise?*

—ALBERTO, PRESIDENT, WEST BANK COLLEGE

IN EDUCATION, ESPECIALLY in the community and technical college sector, we have and will forever take pride in championing the students-first ethos. At the same time, too rarely do we pause to confront the fact that education is also first and foremost about educators themselves—their training and development, sure, but also their well-being, struggles, emotions, joys, and pains. So this chapter is not just about the admirable things done by the people in this book. Equally important, it positions education as an educators-first issue too, with the hope of supporting their full humanity as they deliver on their students-first promise by maintaining the highest levels of care for students—and themselves.

## AN INFLUX OF CHANGE AND INNOVATION

"Part worried, part stunned, part amped up because we knew we had to do things now. So, there's a lot of adrenaline and anxiety," said Renee in response to my question on her initial reactions when the pandemic hit. With a background and training in business and education, Renee has been Keystone College's vice president of academic affairs and faculty development for nearly six years, after having served as associate vice president, dean, associate dean, program director, and faculty. Institutional news sources reveal her to be widely respected and relied upon, and her colleagues describe Renee as a "good captain as the storms ebb and flow" and someone who "really listens" and approaches everyone with "compassion and care." Her decades-long tenure at the college is bolstered by her down-to-earth, democratic way of engaging and working alongside her faculty on a daily basis. Being in the trenches with her faculty, literally, has always been Renee's approach.

But now she must think about how to do that differently, and it is difficult. It felt surreal coming out of her last cabinet meeting in March 2020, in which the president announced that the college was going fully remote and everyone needed to pack up and go remote too. Renee was saying to herself, "I can't be remote. I have to be here. I have to be in the office. I have to meet with my faculty and staff." She walked around the first floor of the college's main building—the airy, open, spacious, and bright design that took the breath away from new students and visitors. But now "they already started to take out tables and put up crime tape to signify what had been cleaned and the place was a ghost town. It was silent. It was starting to get dark. And I think that's when it kind of hit me, like it was so sad. And I was walking down this little hall, right here." Renee pointed to the hallway right by where we sat—still empty and quiet—and said:

> My colleague was with his backpack and his bags from his office, leaving, and I was gonna say goodbye. That's the first time I broke down. I just broke down, sobbing, because the intensity of those two weeks

kind of hit home at the same time the uncertainty of what was coming. And I gathered myself and packed up my stuff and built a home office and on we went. But yeah, thinking back, it was a mix of emotions. And also, we have to do what we have to do. We as executive leaders didn't have time to be emotional or wonder. We just had to do stuff.

They sure did stuff. Just like that, Keystone College where Renee is, along with their peers in the state and across the country, kicked into high gear to adapt and innovate. To give a detailed sense of the range and depth of the efforts implemented, postdoctoral researcher Yen Lee and I zeroed in on a Midwestern state, using text mining techniques and qualitative coding of news media to generate a comprehensive, albeit nonexhaustive, depiction of the various initiatives burgeoning across the state in the short span of a year following the March 2020 shutdown.[1] As depicted in figure 1.1, although efforts varied and fluctuated over time, almost no facet of a community and technical education was left untouched, ranging from access to technology and supplies for virtual learning, to various instructional adaptations, to wide-ranging support for students' mental health and basic needs, and to efforts altering operational procedures, policies, and structures that impeded students' academic progress. It is truly extraordinary to see change occurring at this magnitude. It is not just about how quickly the colleges can add new things, but how swiftly they can change and remove long-existing, taken-for-granted things that amounted to obvious barriers, only now made laser clear during times of crisis.

## DELIVERING PROMISE, PENALTY FREE

Yes, a crisis is often associated with intense difficulty, trouble, and adverse consequences. And the real common driver behind the incredible feats to tackle these challenges, in the words of Wade, president of Nova Technical College, is "penalty free." With a professional background combining psychology, business, and education, Wade had served as an executive vice president and a variety of leadership and teaching roles before assuming

**FIGURE 1.1** Institutional response and adaptations from March 2020 to May 2021

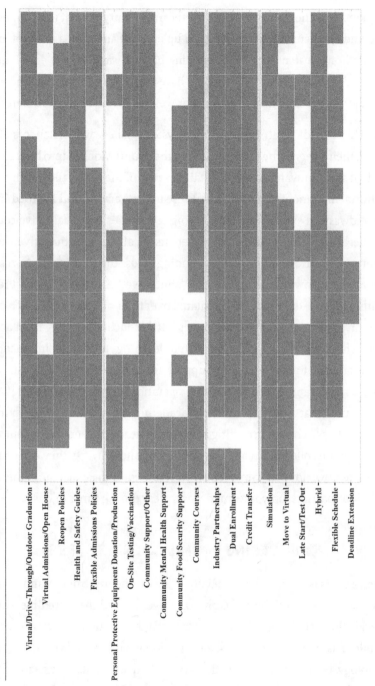

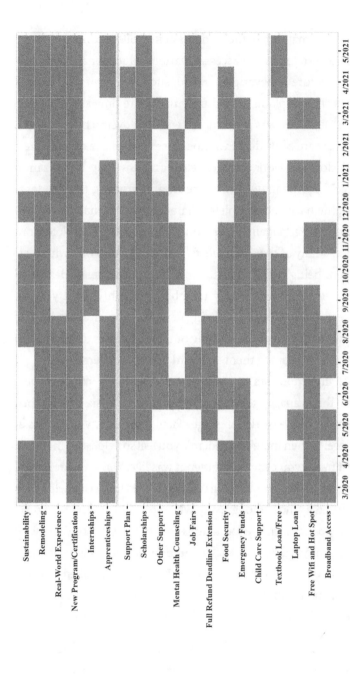

NOTE. Each cell represents occurrence of its corresponding type of institutional response/adaptations (along the *y*-axis) during the corresponding month/year (along the *x*-axis). Darker shading indicates the occurrences of institutional responses/adaptations, and no shading indicates no activities during the given month/year.

the presidency. The majority of the students at the college come from rural areas in the Midwest, for whom access to various educational opportunities and infrastructure is never guaranteed, such as internet bandwidth and computers. This explains why, during the entire time since the outbreak of COVID-19, Wade was preoccupied with one overarching thought: "How do we take care of students who because of all of the outside pressures—school closings, work changes, etc.—can leave the organization as penalty free?" By "penalty free," Wade meant ensuring that students were able to come back and complete whatever they originally set out to achieve without being "penalized for something that was completely out of their control." Many of the educators felt the exact same way, with their primary concern being to help the students stay on course. As described by Virginia, a biotechnology faculty member for twenty-three years at Keystone College: "I don't remember being nervous so much as feeling this pressure that we had to figure something out; our students didn't sign up for that at all, and so, keeping them on board was my concern."

Meanwhile, the educators grappling with this same concern were empowered by their capacity to shift and help during a crisis, as described by Lisa, a member of the world languages faculty for twenty-one years at Keystone College: "When there's a pandemic you feel so helpless sometimes, like there's not much you can do. But then it was like, 'Oh, wait a minute. I can do something. I know how to teach online. I can do this. I can help.'" This realization infused agency among many who altered their long-held practices, structures, policies, and expectations for students to continue with their education amid massive external disruption. Mateo, a faculty member and program director for human services at Keystone, described how the forced transition made him and his colleagues realize both their capacity to be innovative and the glaring inequities that came to the surface:

> Once the pandemic hit, we didn't have a choice, we had to say, we either adapt and try to be creative in how we're teaching our students, or we absorb the consequences, which is gonna be students that are

disengaged and that are not developing a skill set. When push came to shove, we realized that we could do a lot more than we initially thought we could with online teaching and learning where there was still some engagement. We really looked at our policies and practices and said what's working and what's not working. The other part is that clearly, that time opened our eyes so much to all the inequities that we have. Not only around healthcare, but access to technology, to be able to engage with education as well as social service needs. All these things that we had never discussed and all these things that some people were not fully aware of back in 2018.

College staff shared similar concerns and realizations expressed by the faculty. Daniela, an academic support specialist at Ridgeline Technical College for four years, was "hyper-focused" on these interlacing layers of student needs and concerns through her academic support role:

Understanding that people come with gender, economic, cultural duffel bags that impact how they experience the world, and I would say that this very much came into hyperfocus for us when we would be meeting with students. And we were meeting with students not in a safe and quiet place like my office, right? We were meeting in my dining room with my kids chirping around and the dog barking and whatever was going on in their homes, where sometimes there were some issues that we needed to ask about that we were watching happen behind them. We were seeing some pretty precarious situations online where we're worried that it was not going to be enough.

Exactly because of that newly gained awareness of how various inequities manifest in life contexts that directly affect students, these supports put forward are not without their intricate challenges and emotional costs as college staff attempted to alleviate the worsening circumstances among some of the most underserved students. Casey, director of the

Center for Teaching and Learning at Midtown College for the past two years, reflected on how she and those faculty she supported had come face-to-face with the harsh realities of many students' lives on a whole new level. "The suffering and the lack of security that the majority of, frankly, of our students experience on a relatively continual basis. And our college made a lot of good decisions about how to use some of our federal funding directly to help students. But bottom line, you know, our faculty struggle with having students be able to attend remotely, having very chaotic living environments that now became visible for all to see. Some of which could be pretty disturbing. We're just so much more aware of our students' personal lives." Marie, a biology faculty member at Keystone College for seven years, also expressed the toll taken on her staff colleagues in their efforts to support students in as many ways as possible: "It's tough because I know there are students that are struggling.... But when you hear about people that have had real horrible crises or assault, that's traumatizing. I mean it is. So, how do you deal with that? How do you not take it in? Then, how do you keep serving all these students?"

These insights, experiences, and struggles underline the extraordinary feat community and technical college educators undertook that honored the multiple identities, life contexts, and needs of their students. Yet, as whole persons, these same institutional leaders, faculty, advisors, and staff members were also dealing with multiple challenges exacerbated by the pandemic. Running parallel to their commitment to keeping students going took an emotional toll on newer and seasoned educators alike. I already briefly alluded to this through Casey and Marie's insights, but now I turn a brighter light on the educators themselves as whole persons. Over and over again through my interviews, I learned about how these educators coped, struggled, persisted, and collapsed, and just as much about how they also acted with swiftness, innovation, and flexibility, all the while delivering on their promise to put students first.

## FIRED UP AND BURNED OUT: HOW THE EDUCATORS EXPERIENCED THE PANDEMIC

"How are we going to continue delivering on our promise?" This was Alberto's first reaction to the pandemic. As president and an executive leader, Alberto was all about delivering promise against extraordinary challenges. Identifying as a Latino man, Alberto was a campus president at a community college in the South while having already accepted a job offer, pre-COVID-19, as president of one of the community colleges in the Midwest. For a while, he was practically doing two different top leadership roles simultaneously, which turned his entire transition upside down: the sheer volume of doing two jobs, which was extra challenging; social isolation experienced by his entire family; the death of his father, to whom he didn't get to say a proper goodbye because of social distancing; and the "subtle" racism he endured as a person of color in the Midwest. Halfway through our interview, Alberto broke down in tears, lowering his head while apologizing for not sharing information that was "helpful or positive." It was the first time, he later shared, that he was able to pause and reflect on how these compounding challenges adversely affected his holistic health: "As it is right now, mentally I really don't have much more capacity. Healthwise in this period of time, I'm heavier than I've ever been. I'm a lot more depressed than I've ever been. I'm usually a very light-hearted person. Nowadays I just come home and go sit in our basement by myself just to decompress. It's been taxing."

But then, as an executive leader, the new president of his college, Alberto recognized the paradox of where he's positioned socio-geo-organizationally: "Being here where America's race reckoning is occurring has been tough and then, as a leader of color, to use your platform to try and get movement and get people to realize and make changes that are necessary." Toward that goal, Alberto started a project with a focus on having radical conversations around race and equity using the arts—as a compelling commonality that could bring the community together. This innovation was especially poignant in a college and surrounding community that is primarily Black and Hmong, along with racial injustices happening right in their backyard and amplified by the pandemic. To address the division and inequities, the project aimed to develop programming that showcases art, music, and storytelling by local youth as a way to bring people together through highlighting diverse arts in the area. Plus, the project was a way to support and sustain equity through community relationships and physical structures in the form of a center. Alberto's story illustrates the ever-difficult, ever-critical, and ever-compounding work of addressing racial equity as both an institutional leader and a person of color in the racialized and racializing social context in which he lives. Although he is passionate about "fighting for change," it can often feel like "ice skating up a hill." As a result, Alberto's energy, which used to feel unlimited, runs up against the significant weight and tension that come with engaging in these efforts.

Beyond executive leaders, the faculty and staff were certainly not immune from this dual reality of being both *fired up and burned out* at the same time. The immediate interlacing impact and responsibility were certainly felt by faculty. David was exactly positioned to view things through that lens. Coming from a family of educators, and with his own educational and professional background in math and education, David was serving as department chair and faculty at a community college in the South at the onset of the pandemic. David knew all too well the energy needed to drive important efforts for the college and the exhaustion that could ensue from reconciling too many responsibilities for both him and his faculty members. "In my mind, what was going on with all these different initiatives that were going at a time that in our minds required everyone being on site? How would that continue? Continuity of learning was important. Then really instantly, what superseded that was family and well-being. Was our faculty going to be OK? I started thinking about their families and their children. How this abrupt change to their lives will impact how they function."

David was right. Although many of the faculty I interviewed willingly strive to give their all to students, the pandemic introduced, and in some cases exposed, the deep exhaustion that could snuff out even the most galvanized faculty. Esther, an early childhood education faculty member at Lakefront College in the Midwest for twelve years, was initially fired up as someone who can "personally thrive with a little pressure on." While many of her colleagues were burned out, Esther felt she could still go on—until she couldn't, when she got to a point where she "no longer had any resources to offer." She went on, sounding helpless: "I was at a loss, and nobody else knew what to do either, basically." Esther's burnout as an instructor who is typically on the go came from a pandemic-imposed new reality that is even more high-pressure, high-stakes, and always evolving. It reveals a troubling theme that all this burnout can occur without people being cognizant of it happening, or in many cases, realizing it much later. "What can be alarming is when people don't realize they are burning out and they keep pushing themselves," said Kayla, a nursing faculty member for seventeen years at Midtown College.

## WHEN EQUITY WORK IS PART OF THE EQUATION

Further complicating the dual reality of fired up and burned out is the hard work of centering equity as a steady thread in day-to-day work. Alberto's story is both inspiring and somber—inspiring for the innovative ways in which he aims to weave equity into the very fabric of his college and the local community; and somber because his story sits right at the intersection of racial battle fatigue and the mixed sense of burden, responsibility, and commitment that come with doing equity work on persons of color within obstinate institutional climates and cultures. A term coined by William Smith, "racial battle fatigue" has grown out of extensive research on the mental, emotional, and physical stressors of racism and their cumulative effects on the coping, health, and well-being of people of color.[2] Much of this work focuses on students and faculty, although leaders of color like Alberto experience these same challenges. Equity work as an already uphill battle is even more taxing for educators of color, who often, unlike their white counterparts, are expected to be a voice for equity and a critical source of support for students of color who experience racism. In Alberto's case, racial battle fatigue, burnout, and his ever-present commitment to equity-centered leadership converged to create difficult-to-resolve internal tensions and conflicts.

This exact conundrum puts those on the front lines championing equity work, whether executive leaders or not, into a precarious state of severe burnout. From closely working with those involved in equity initiatives across the state, Claudia sounded the alarm:

> I think the biggest burnout that I've seen of all the groups I work with is the diversity, equity, and inclusion group, a collection of highly skilled people who were highly in tune with what was going on with students who did not feel heard. The amount of work, like physical and emotional work that that group is being asked to do has not changed and has increased. And so, combining the COVID-19 pandemic with racial violence that continues, people in those positions are just constantly on. Helping students, supporting students, the ones who are going to lead something and respond to something. So that's the group I think I've personally seen the most burnout and turn over with.

These are the people enacting the countless efforts behind the volume and richness of the adaptations illustrated in figure 1.1, and their efforts are dynamic, steady, and never-ending. Without taking away from the massive difficulties experienced by students who were already living in challenging contexts, the educators were also caught between a taxing reality of their own and the endless support that many continue to render to the students. This new duality led to dual struggles experienced by faculty, staff, and leaders. And a reframing of support for every person—students and educators alike—is in dire need. As Ali, vice president of learning at Midtown College, put it, "We really struggled certain ways. We lost some faculty, we lost some students, and we lost some staff as a result, and so on. But you know, honestly, before we start talking about doing new things like technology, you really have to show compassionate support for these people, you really have to understand their needs."

And yet there is a conspicuous absence of support for faculty and staff—the very educators who carry the bulk of the responsibility for serving students. As an example, if we take a closer look at the numerous changes adopted by colleges in a Midwestern state as depicted in figure 1.1, we may notice this lack of support for educators as reflected on college websites and in media sources. Although this does not definitively demonstrate a lack of *existence* of such supports, what is being communicated, albeit imperfectly, can reveal to some extent priorities in efforts and resources. Against the volume of student-centered efforts *by* the educators is the strikingly little to no effort *for* the educators, a theme emerging out of our text mining analysis that was largely confirmed by my interviews with the educators themselves. There are shining examples that were exceptions to this norm, and I unpack some of the most insightful stories, observations, and innovations in chapter 6 of the book.

"How are we going to continue delivering on our promise?" As I was writing this book, I was reminded of Alberto's question countless times, and every time it took on a new layer of nuance and impact. I realized that unbeknownst to me when I first heard it, and perhaps to him when he first articulated it, the question implores all of us in education to pause and ponder, and if we do that hard and long enough, we may recognize that the *how* is as much with students at heart as it is with educators at heart. When we talk about humanity and compassion in teaching and student support, which I will get to in chapters 2 and 3, we must think about the people who are serving the students, especially in the community and technical college context. These institutions offer some of the most complex conditions to work in, with their faculty, advisors, and other staff often expected to do more with less. They take on heavy teaching loads, advise hundreds or even thousands of students, support some of the most vulnerable populations, and have limited access to professional development, all the while often operating with scarce resources.[3]

These educators, in their attempts to be everything to everyone, albeit imperfectly, strive to deliver promise to their students, often with their own humanity taking a back seat. The many times I heard these stories and sometimes saw the tears (in person or over Zoom), I left the interviews feeling deeply inspired and yet deeply concerned. Yes, the students-first ethos was widely shared and practiced, but institutions can't sustain what they are built for if humanity-grounded efforts and care are *not* bestowed to the educators first and foremost. In the end, no lasting changes and innovations are enabled by a constant state of feeling committed and being fired up—which is more of a recipe for burnout. This chapter serves as a reminder of that throughout this entire book, and I come back to this topic with a call to action in chapter 6.

## QUESTIONS FOR REFLECTION

- What can be learned from the experiences and resilience of educators during the COVID-19 pandemic?
- What structures and supports can be implemented to address the systemic inequities in access to technology, mental health support, and basic needs for students from historically marginalized communities?
- What policies and funding initiatives are needed to strengthen the infrastructure and resources to address equity gaps?
- How can educators center equity in their daily work while doing it collaboratively to minimize individual or collective burnout?

- At the organizational level, what initiatives can be implemented to develop community and shared responsibility for well-being?
- What factors contribute to effective educational innovations and adaptations, taking into account the diverse needs and circumstances of students and educators alike?
- What does a students-first *and* educators-first institutional culture look like?

# 2

## Compassion-Enhanced
## Teaching Innovations

*Without diluting their education, how do we lend compassion and grace?*

—LISA, FACULTY MEMBER, KEYSTONE COLLEGE

"I REMEMBER THE first class that I had synchronous when I had started the Zoom meeting. I was just facing a black blank page. All the students turned off their cameras. I was just surprised that I am looking at a very blank black page and had to teach to them." That jarring feeling when switching from his classroom to a virtual environment was still so vivid two years later for Behi, an engineering technology faculty member at Ridgeline Technical College. While he felt that he was ready to pivot, when the reality hit, so did the shock, as he was so used to—and cherished—his experience with students in the same physical room: "Looking at them eye-to-eye, speaking with them." For those who were used to teaching in labs, such as Brad, a manufacturing faculty member at Prairie College, the switch was even more jarring. Not only was he accustomed to hands-on labs and using tactile objects during his entire teaching career, but many of his students—those enrolled in technical and technician

35

programs—"didn't even know how to use Word or Canvas, so it was challenging that way."

For students in community and technical colleges, the classroom acts as the primary (and often the sole) college scene, and what happens or doesn't happen in the classroom is vital to their entire college experience and any measure of success.[1] Because of that, the pandemic disruptions to classroom teaching and learning hit in a most direct, intense, and high-stakes manner. No facets of teaching and learning were left untouched, and the disruptions across lecture rooms/halls, labs, or workshops were felt, experienced, and negotiated by everyone, virtually and pun intended. In the meantime, the shock these instructors experienced also marked the onboarding of an unexpected new journey of teaching and learning. For Brad, without the shiny props and equipment of in-person labs, he was forced to explore software and simulators like never before. But that wasn't enough. Brad took a deep look at how he was teaching in light of the vastly different levels of student readiness for a virtual environment: "That made me look at my teaching style. So I had to look at different ways to be able to get my point across without relying on these props that I've been using. My delivery method was something that I had to work on a little bit to be able to get my point across to just different types of people, so everyone had the same opportunities to do well in the class regardless of their background." Behi shared strikingly similar experiences: "So I started working to find every appropriate method or approach to reach the students, give them [a] wide range of accessibility to different types of materials."

## COMPASSION AS GROUNDING TEXTURE
## FOR TEACHING INNOVATIONS

The instructors' revelations as such set into motion a series of teaching innovations, online or not—many of which are poised to be carried far into the future. Before getting into the specifics, though, I am moved to share that, when asked about new or innovative practices, the most stand-out thread was *compassion*, a word shared by faculty spanning nearly all programs—liberal arts; science, technology, engineering, and mathematics (STEM) majors; technical and technician training programs; and developmental education. It is something that seems so simple and basic, and yet so rarely a formalized thread underlying teaching and learning—until a public health crisis cut right across layers of norms and presumptions about how to teach and touched the deepest humanity in everyone. Take Peder, a graphic design faculty member at Glacier Technical College, for example. In his twenty-six years at the college, he was used to instructors taking a more rigid approach to their teaching and interactions with students. Yet he noticed that the pandemic provoked a "softening" of practices across instructors, including himself. When navigating this softening, Peder highlighted the importance of "showing grace to the stress that we put on our learners in some way and trying to figure out a way to not dilute their education while we're showing them that grace." Reflecting on these changes, he said, "I think that's the most nontechnological innovation that we're able to bring to the table."

Other instructors also noted a transformation in how they interacted and conversed with students that reflected greater compassion, such as William, a journalism faculty member at Keystone College for twenty-five years: "I used the word 'love' in my responses to them more than I've ever done before. I have said that 'I love your work this week.' I never ever before the pandemic ever used the word 'love,' ever." William continued to provide specific, constructive feedback on various aspects of students' work, but adding "love" to his vocabulary was entirely new, and yet it felt so natural: "I use that because I feel love for my students, and I feel that the pandemic just brought that out manyfold. It's just this deep concern. And at the same time, I guess I just tried to be more of a human being in the remote environment. But at the same time, we so respect our students for their endurance and for their hope for themselves, and it's just such an honor to be a teacher, but it's specifically during the pandemic and because our students were going through so much."

While compassion is not something that can be formally operationalized in precise ways as part of instruction, it is one of the most powerful forces that compelled the faculty to change and innovate out of support, empathy, love, and respect for their students. It undergirds the various teaching innovations that I detail next across instructional platforms and throughout the ups, downs, and pivots over the past few years.

## LEARNINGS FROM PANDEMIC-AFFECTED INSTRUCTION, ONLINE AND BEYOND

The instructors in my book were invariably awakened to a whole new dimension of teaching and learning that stirred up grace, humanity, and compassion, all against the backdrop of the simultaneously familiar and enigmatic online instructional environment they were thrust into. Therefore, in this chapter on teaching innovations, I must devote the first part to online instruction. To do that, a few cautionary notes are in order. The pandemic context may have made it appear that, all of a sudden, everyone was engaging in online teaching and learning in an unprecedented manner. Headlines such as "Don't Kid Yourself: Online Lectures Are Here to Stay," in the *New York Times*, and "Virtual Learning Might Be the Best Thing to Happen to Schools," in *The Atlantic*, dominated the media, along with institutional communications highlighting the numerous virtual learning, courses, and program offerings.[2] But that is too simplistic a portrayal of a far more enduring and complicated phenomenon. For one thing, online instruction isn't entirely new to the community college scene; well before the pandemic, at least half of community college students had taken an online class.[3] These institutions offer online classes out of their primary concern for the expediency and convenience that the larger community college student population needs: students who concurrently balance numerous things going on in their lives, working full time, raising children, giving care to family or significant others, and the list goes on.

But despite its long existence in service to student access, online instruction has not lived up to its potential in terms of successful learning outcomes. Students tend to have lower grades in online courses than in face-to-face ones, with Black and Latinx students more adversely affected.[4] More often than not, online classes have failed to create the kinds of motivational environments that help students persist and perform to their highest potential—ones that build connections and cultivate students' agency, autonomy, and self-efficacy. This conundrum reflects the same inertia I described earlier in the introduction to this book—that access often does not translate into the fully delivered promise of the wide range of student outcomes across motivational, academic, and educational domains.

Further muddling this paradox is that the sudden pivot toward *online platforms* does not necessarily equate *online teaching and learning*; rather, it is more a matter of coping in the mode of crisis management. As sociologist Tressie McMillan-Cottom incisively argued, postsecondary institutions currently lack the infrastructure, resources, and training that need to be in place for engaging in such a sweeping, systemic evolution toward pedagogically sound online teaching and learning.[5] This is true for already well-resourced institutions, let alone persistently underfunded institutions like community and technical colleges. So the reality facing all instructors is this: for those already engaging in online instruction, the perennial challenges they have faced carried over and appeared graver than ever, as the pandemic precisely affected those traditional online populations the most; for those new to online classes, they don't have already existing, well-thought-out systems, structures, and training to rely on. These instructors, along with their institutions, were all in survival mode in the initial phase of pandemic-affected online instruction.

## Innovating the Structure: Continuity, Stability, and Clarity

Survival mode also inspires and allows instructors—whether new to or familiar with online instruction—to turn the corner, learning, developing, or revising online teaching approaches and strategies, like those briefly previewed in Brad's and Behi's examples. Now take a more in-depth look at Shawn, whom we met in the introduction of this book. After the initial phase of disbelief and scrambling sunk in, Shawn, who had not taught online before, quickly grasped some of the things that would lend him and his students as much continuity, stability, and clarity as possible. To infuse a sense of *continuity* of learning and ameliorate disruption to the greatest possible extent, he approached his online lectures to mimic the structure and schedule of what classes were like in person. Extending beyond minimizing disruption, continuity is an enduringly impactful element in structuring online courses, as it helps scaffold—that is, ease students through building blocks from session to session and week to week. The essence of continuity was reflected in other instructors' approaches to structuring their online courses as well, such as William's six steps—review previous content, present new content, engage materials in-depth, explore new ideas, test understanding, and synthesize key learnings—so that students know what to expect and build on their learning on a daily and weekly basis. "Then the next week begins. Well, what happens? You go back to step one. And the cycle continues," William explained.

*Stability* is another aspect to which Shawn assigned a new meaning—stable access to learning difficult science materials that don't need to be rushed. Shawn admitted that, for as long as he taught, one of the biggest assumptions embedded in science teaching was the unquestioned need for "struggling to get through all this content." Having to put the content online propelled Shawn to realize that, first, he didn't have to rush the content against an oft-assumed delimited class time, because now "students can go in and view those as often and whenever they want to." Second, this stability for both him and his students allowed Shawn to reflect and be creative: "Now I can take a step back and focus more on specific areas and addressing areas where students are having trouble, and not feel that 'Oh, I gotta get through all this content before the session ends.'" Shawn took stability in access to the next level by creating interactive and open spaces so that students could regularly engage him and one another. Just like that, stable access to science materials led to the next level of stable access to instructor and peer support—something of extraordinary impact and yet rare in the old model, dominated by the unquestioned sense of rush against limited time.

*Clarity* in content organization also matters, realized Dave, an agriculture faculty member at Nova Technical College. Although he had taught at the college for eight years, the pandemic shed new light on how to structure a supportive online environment, particularly around course content organization and guidance: "I think one of the things that stood out is when you convert things to online, you have to be much, much more careful in your descriptions, verbal, recorded, and written, in order for a student to do an assignment well. Online learning students will be much quicker to say, 'I don't get that' because they don't get to hear the in-person explanation, so you have to do a better job with the descriptions and details." Without naming it, Dave's vision and practice for clarity embody some of the key elements of universal design for learning (UDL), where multiple means of engagement, representation, and action and expression are used so that all students have the opportunity to participate in meaningful learning.[6]

Back to William. He emphasized the importance of structuring his courses with clarity underscored by simplicity, having content organized in folders, along with guidance on how to navigate them: "All these different steps need to be clearly defined. This is something that's really important. The organization in remote education is top, top, top priority. It's this simplicity in the organization that is absolutely critical." Clarity, as rendered by instructors like Dave and William, served as a key ingredient underlying a more even playing field for students through transparent and explicit direction and explanation, as well as access to learning and content in an online space.

## Innovating the Practice: Presence, Flexibility, and Proactivity

Innovations to the course structure, especially for online courses, were bolstered by the rich meaning that faculty assigned to the structure through changing old practices and developing new ones. Lisa, a world languages instructor, knows far too well that learning really occurs only when both the instructor and students are fully present. She strove to invite her students' presence into her online class through her imperfect, authentic *presence*: "Don't worry about those perfect videos. Nobody wants to watch those. Students would much prefer that you drop your pencil, that your dog starts barking. It's more interesting. You have to go 'Hold on.' I mean that's much more human." Lisa's idea that we can humanize the online class through bringing in the instructor's genuine, messy reality can take away some of the fear and unease of an online setting devoid of in-person connectivity.

Lisa also developed new approaches that prioritize *flexibility* in course content and student choices. She provided materials for students to choose among that would achieve the intended learning objectives but give them an opportunity to take ownership of their learning and interests: "I had four readings for them to read, and I would say like, 'Just choose your own adventure. Pick two.' So, they still can get just as much learning out of those two as they did out of those four. Then we can have a little fun with it, student voice and choice." Liz, a math faculty member at Rapids Trail College, embraced flexibility by adjusting the course content to reflect the programs her students were in, like health fields, chemistry, or business, so that the students could obtain core skills and knowledge in ways that supported their individual contexts: "We had to really focus in on what truly does matter here. All of that stuff that we do in this course doesn't matter, so we're like OK, for these students, we're not gonna do that. We have to boil this down to what matters. You can have that mathematics that's going to help you be successful in what's next." This added flexibility by Lisa, Liz, and other instructors gave students the freedom to take control of and stay engaged with their education.

*Proactivity* is another element underlying the new approaches that many instructors adopted. For Dave, it meant progress monitoring and proactive outreach to ensure students were on track before it was too late, as online students tend to disappear more easily, given that they often perceive or experience a limited sense of connection and support from instructors in virtual environments.[7] Dave introduced frequent assessments—but ungraded—so he could stay in tune with students' learning to determine whether he needed to revisit content or concepts: "Two and a half years ago, I was not a big fan of quizzes. I didn't use a lot of quizzes. That just wasn't my style. Now, I'm doing them more online. It helps me understand what the students are retaining or if something wasn't explained well, but also then I go back and re-explain the answers of the quizzes." Dave's proactivity was also reflected in outreach to students in the form of short video clips or online text messaging through a tool called Pronto. These proactive approaches allowed him to stay closely attuned to students' progress in learning and keep them connected in the online classroom.

But proactivity can also mean a more introspective way of thinking on the part of the instructor. As Shawn engaged in changing some of his practices, *predictability* adds a subtle subdimension to proactivity. That is, to anticipate and address some of the challenges or mistakes that students might make in a virtual setting, unfamiliar to both him and the students, and "be pretty proactive about it." Shawn reflected on how his emerging approaches were in fact rooted in his long understanding of the student population he works with—largely first-generation, low-income students who often need and thrive on proactive academic support: "So, teaching at a community college, anything that you create for the benefit of students, you have to first show them how to use it correctly; and second, you have to imagine how they will use it *incorrectly*, or they will totally negate the benefits." There is an even deeper motivation behind

Shawn's proactivity in predicting what could go wrong to prevent the consequences of the mistakes. Within the larger community college student population, there are subgroups of students who are further disadvantaged in challenging contexts. In Shawn's words, "those who perhaps don't have the best home environment that's conducive for studying for various reasons or put more at risk because they're less able to remove themselves from that situation."

These are the resounding themes from the experiments and victories of the instructors I talked to. Without all faculty necessarily naming or knowing the research behind their own practices, these defining elements are aligned with what experts of online education, like Claire Major, Kathryn Linder, Stephanie Blackmon, Katrina Meyer, and others, found to be essential to setting up the course structure, content, and support for a successful online learning experience.[8] Particularly important to highlight here is an online course quality rubric developed at the height of the pandemic by educational researcher Di Xu and colleagues—an evidence-based tool that reflects many of the practices emerging among the faculty I interviewed.[9] In fact, long before the pandemic, these practices were rigorously researched with well-documented evidence, but far less rigorously practiced among instructors who taught online. At one level, Shawn and many of his peers seemed to have stumbled upon these practices, compelled by the pandemic context. At a far deeper level, based on what didn't work even before the pandemic, both the instructors and their students were ready for a reimagined online experience that encapsulated these and other high-impact practices. Shawn's reflective observations about the misassumptions of having to pack lots of science content into one session speak to the long-held experiential knowledge among instructors like himself about both the challenges their students were facing and what hadn't worked in their teaching practices. As expressed by Shawn and reflected in his students' positive feedback, his new practices eliminated some of the most stubborn challenges they experienced during normal times. "Um, they liked the interactivity. They like that they can get the questions asked and answered in real time. They don't have to send an email and wait for me to respond, and they like the accessibility." Intriguingly, these are the students who often need intensive coaching with study habits, ideally in an in-person environment; and yet Shawn and others showed a way to accomplish that within a virtual setting, made possible by infusing continuity, stability, clarity, presence, flexibility, and proactivity into online teaching and learning environments.

These adjustments by the instructors to restructure and redo their online courses may seem small, incidental, and in some cases forced without a choice. But for many instructors, they are pivotal innovations that positively shaped how their students experience imposed online learning through a revised structure that is continuous, stable, and clear, all supported by instructors' efforts to be ever more present, flexible, and proactive. While structure and practice aren't everything and there is so much more to the curriculum and the larger pedagogy—which I will get to next— these seemingly minor things represent an enormous step toward online teaching and learning with an equity lens in the context of community and technical colleges. They give concrete meaning to access and support—not just the rhetoric or idea or even commitment, but rather the types of access and support that matter for most of the students at these institutions, who spend every day burdened with reconciling multiple responsibilities and situations in achieving their educational goals. The innovations tried by the instructors point to a new possibility for these very students to truly and fully participate in an education that better reflects *their* realities.

## BEYOND STRUCTURE AND PRACTICE: TOWARD THE LARGER *HOW* AND *WHAT* OF TEACHING INNOVATIONS

These innovative practices and ideas emerging from pandemic-imposed online teaching transcend the confines of modalities and have enduring implications. Growing out of a deep compassion for students during crisis, they reflect the faculty's responsiveness, creativity, and resource-fulness. For the individual instructors, they often felt that their efforts were pragmatic, out of necessity, and thus not "big enough." But they set the perfect stage for a larger, bolder vision of teaching innovations in community and technical colleges. I turn to this discussion now.

## The *How* of Teaching Innovations: Asset-Based and Trauma-Informed

The urgent desire to infuse more compassion into teaching had faculty trying new approaches and practices that they had never adopted before. Most of them were compelled to engage in these unfamiliar practices as a way to render compassion, as they saw students struggling with challenging life contexts and limited access to resources that prevented them from demonstrating learning in the traditional way. Polly, a nursing educator at Keystone College, learned to use narrative pedagogy to center the "big realities" of her students: "The number one thing I've learned how to do is narrative pedagogy, so just absolutely bringing in the students to tell their stories, bringing faculty to tell their stories, telling stories that I hear from people, that's probably been the most powerful tool that I have sort of learned to utilize, of them all." Narrative pedagogy originates from the field of nursing and focuses on learning as a partnership between educators and students, sharing, analyzing, and interpreting their lived experiences toward interrogating and reforming existing practices.[10] By adopting narrative pedagogy, Polly centered students' voices to guide her instruction, "meeting people where they're at and walking with them." Casey, director of the Center for Teaching and Learning at Midtown College, saw an uptake of similar new teaching approaches among her faculty colleagues, from as simple as using more student-centered language to bringing students as experts into the process of course development—"the full collaborative, either assignments, or syllabus design where they actually allow their students to help them create their assignments or their deadlines or their assessments."

Serendipitously, what Polly and many other instructors experimented with reflects small elements of the broader family of asset-based pedagogies that represent a transformative repertoire. In a nutshell, asset-based pedagogies and educational approaches are culturally affirming, relevant, and sustaining approaches stemming from core theories and concepts such as culturally relevant pedagogy by Gloria Ladson-Billings, culturally sustaining pedagogy by Django Paris and H. Samy Alim, community cultural wealth by Tara Yosso, funds of knowledge by Norma González and Luis Moll, and validation theory by Laura Rendón.[11] While asset-based pedagogies were brought to light years ago by prominent scholars of color, given the agility of whiteness permeating all levels of education, their adoption has been a slow-moving process and their core concepts and ideas still seemed new to faculty. Polly captured this in her reflections: "My understanding regarding inclusive, equitable teaching and practice is definitely still evolving. It is definitely something that is for those of us at that frontline engagement level, we recognize that it's too diffuse and it needs to be more formalized." Yet those faculty who willingly moved out of their comfort zone and toward centering student assets and strengths, many of them being white educators, shone a light on how asset-based pedagogies and practices could become a common reality in the teaching enterprise at community and technical colleges— institutions with a history of being attuned to their diverse student populations and communities.[12]

Moving toward asset-based pedagogies must also come with a deep sensitivity to the collective and individual trauma that is an inseparable part of education, particularly in the community college context, where students experience higher incidences of trauma.[13] Indeed, a few of the faculty and instructional support staff I interviewed have become well versed in and started to practice trauma-informed pedagogy, but these faculty were rare. Still, I want to highlight a shining exception: Daniela, an academic support specialist who manages the Learning Center as part of Ridgeline Technical College's library and academic support services. She is highly trusted and lauded as an expert leading faculty and staff development with trauma-informed pedagogy, having published work on this very topic. As a trauma survivor herself, Daniela's approaches were always couched in how safe relationships affect the learning environment. As the pandemic context, complicated by political turmoil and racial justice upheavals, put existing relationships between students and teachers to the test, Daniela realized that the value of trauma-informed care for students of color, especially Black students, was "just underlined and bold faced." She saw a real risk that existing relationships would break if faculty did not recognize the importance of trauma-informed work: "And this is certainly in the time of Black Lives Matter just really coming to the national attention, and we have so many students who were just deeply pained by that. People really hurting and really angry and recognizing that all of a sudden, the nation is seeing their pain for the first time and not quite knowing what to do with that, and how that relates to school."

Under these turbulent circumstances, some instructors, despite their best intentions, asked students to write about police brutality against Black people, a subject that could be trauma-inducing, according to Daniela: "I mean there was so much that was relating, and students might be asked to write about it, and it was so fresh. It's like, how do you write about a murder that you just watched when you haven't figured out how you feel about that yet? Coming up with words to participate in a class when you're being asked to process your deepest fear and your deepest pain that you carried around quietly for so long?" So she worked with those faculty, helping them understand and tap into the role that trauma plays in shaping educational experiences, especially those from racially minoritized communities: "There is the safety piece, the transparency piece, that peer support, and voice and choice. Look at some of these assignments, consider giving options or reword them because you're opening doors that are painful for people, and they don't feel like they can participate. People don't need to bleed their hearts out to you in order to pass the class."

Daniela saw this trauma brought to light by the pandemic as an undercurrent that was always there for Black students and others from racially minoritized communities. Her depiction of the challenges and her own innovative approaches lay down the difficult yet promising journey ahead. To further encourage faculty to enhance their teaching approaches with a trauma-informed lens, one impactful approach that Daniela uses is to ask how instructors define their own professional value: "My professional value isn't only linked to how hard my classes, and how smart my students have to be to pass my class. My value is in my kindness. My value is in my ability to lift somebody up so that they can grab a bar and lift themselves the rest of the way. That, that is my value. I think that the talking pretty real with other teachers about that is important. You know, why did we go into this? Why do we go into this job?" Daniela walks her talk. Through interviews with a number of her colleagues and reading a chapter she wrote on trauma-informed academic support, I got further glimpses into her work that is anchored in her professional value and practice.[14] It is a way of educating that recognizes trauma, embraces strengths, and nurtures relationships.

Daniela's example speaks to trauma-informed work as inherently challenging. It grows out of a national focus and efforts around public health, crisis response, and well-being through entities and organizations like the Centers for Disease Control and Prevention's Office of Public Health Preparedness and Response and the Substance Abuse and Mental Health Services Administration's National Center for Trauma-Informed Care.[15] Six principles underline a trauma-informed approach: (1) safety of the physical setting and interactions toward feeling physically and psychologically safe; (2) trustworthiness and transparency to build and maintain trust; (3) peer support among those with shared experiences to promote recovery and healing; (4) collaboration and mutuality to ensure shared power and decision-making; (5) empowerment, voice, and choice to center strengths and experiences toward decision-making and control over healing and recovery; and (6) cultural, historical, and gender issues like stereotypes, biases, and historical trauma are recognized and addressed. A trauma-informed approach represents a promising direction for teaching innovations at community and technical colleges, especially given their long-standing missions of access and reaching some of the most overlooked and underserved students. In this sense, these institutions, with the guidance of trauma-informed practices, stand as a beacon of hope for those with traumatic experiences, pandemic-induced or not.

Asset-based and trauma-informed pedagogies are compelling yet daunting. They require more than a few pages of tips and insights, but the work can start by making small changes that add up to big ones. In Daniela's words, "what we can do is look at some things that are true, about an equitable or a justice-based classroom environment, and say, let me choose that one thing, what can I do? Let me take one of my assignments. Can I make this assignment fit with a justice environment, a justice thread, something. And how can I make the steps one at a time until all of a sudden, I looked at my curriculum? I've looked at who I'm teaching and whose voices and experiences I am choosing to broadcast, or to focus on." If faculty engage with those small, incremental, and yet pivotal moments enough times, they are more likely to arrive at the moment of real pedagogical change that is, in the words of Daniela, "trauma informed, culturally responsive, and poverty informed."

### The *What* of Teaching Innovations: Decolonizing the Curriculum and Content

Contrary to conventional wisdom, I chose to discuss the *what* to teach after the *how*, as apparently the *what* is even slower to change. The *what*—curriculum and content—continues to be a stubborn area of inertia in teaching innovations. Faculty are often resistant to curriculum reform due to their prior (lack of) training, inherited beliefs, assumptions, and expectations about what counts as "rigorous" content, and the interests, power, and authority wielded as part of curriculum control.[16] Thus, while many of the faculty I interviewed were receptive to innovating the *how*— teaching practices, approaches, or even pedagogy—by and large, they held fast to the systems of knowledge embedded in the curriculum and related components. But still, some instructors took small steps toward not only changing *how* they teach, but *what* they teach. Take Esther, an early childhood education faculty member at Lakefront College, as an example. She "used to run a really tight ship with rigid content and policies." During the pandemic, she changed her curriculum and content to be timely, meaningful, and relevant by adopting "a lot of innovative ideas about how to get students through when they can't actually be in the field." For instance, tapping into her professional community nationally, she replaced the old content with "really quality video clips that students could analyze and make meaningful case studies." Looking back, Esther admitted that the pandemic forced her to explicitly name the fact that the rigidity in her course content and approaches could act as stressors for students—something she always had an inkling of but never acted on before: "I kind of thought a lot more about the mental health aspect of things, and I don't want to add more stress with the courses I teach to my students' lives. I've always thought about those types of things, but now I put it into action in my courses if that makes sense. But I wasn't reflecting on that in the way that I was now, and I changed that. Now I feel like I'm practicing what I preach more. It was a lot of work, but it really led to just thinking outside the box and it was a cool outcome."

Changing the *what* to teach also involves instructors evaluating their own curricula to determine whether they foster learning or merely create barriers to students' education. Ashley, a psychology instructor at Skyview Technical College, reflected on how the pandemic helped her recognize the often-excessive requirements that were there simply to "justify the classes instead of delivering the course in a way that was meeting people where they are personally, cognitively, and emotionally." So she stripped away some of the course materials and requirements, which she now views as unnecessary to essential learning objectives in this new light. Her creativity and boldness received positive responses from her students, who described the relief they felt and the joy of learning—often students who were already feeling the heavy weight of compounding challenges. The learning was "grounded" and collective, with students feeling that they were "all in this together," Ashley recalled.

Lisa was similarly sparked to revisit her course content to better serve and truly see her students: "I just brought this renewed effort again, like not only about the pandemic, but like let's make sure that our racial diversity, that our socioeconomic diversity, that all these different diversities we have are reflected in our course materials, because everybody needs to be seen." Without Lisa or other faculty necessarily being able to name them, these practices mirror potential elements—albeit small and incremental—toward the long process of decolonizing teaching, learning, and the curriculum.[17] It means actively challenging and dismantling the entrenched colonial powers, structures, and practices that have influenced education, as well as centering the voices and perspectives of historically marginalized groups and elevating their contributions within the curriculum. Based on what I shared earlier, my participants showed a significant willingness to engage in self-reflection and confront power dynamics embedded in their curricula. They also expressed a readiness to integrate diverse perspectives, cultures, and values into their teaching. While they have a long way to go in the process of decolonization, these steps are crucial, gradual ones for more equity-minded teaching practices in community and technical colleges where faculty and student demographics are still a mismatch, with students of color being served by a largely white faculty.[18] Because of this, it is all the more crucial that faculty reflect on what their curricula are really doing for students (or not) and the ways that they can revisit and simplify the *how* and *what* to achieve a high-quality and transformative educational experience for all.

## COMPASSION: A SPIRIT AND MENTALITY
## WITHOUT DILUTING STUDENTS' EDUCATION

Engaging in these types of innovation in the curriculum and pedagogy in sustained, systemic ways is challenging, to say the least. As shared by the faculty themselves, the practices they started to change or adopt often deviated from a long history of doing instruction in certain ways. Compassion as induced by the pandemic serves as a propellant, and a commitment to compassion seems to make sense and is a relatively easy pitch, but the education of community and technical college students is a far more complex enterprise, given their diverse range of interests, levels of engagement, and motivation, let alone the sheer fact that many are first-generation students who need more than compassion to guide them through their college careers. As Lisa put it: "How do we lend compassion and grace without diluting their education?" Lisa's sentiment speaks to a multifaceted theme of faculty engaging in trial, error, and ongoing reflective adaptations in their quest to balance what students *want* versus what they *need*. Faculty wrestled with how to honor students' own wants while providing sufficient, on-point support for what they need for their education; how to accommodate flexibilities in student attendance modes while ensuring a high-quality experience; and how to assess, respond to, and positively influence the engagement styles of the students who experienced the pandemic shock.

Michelle, a chemistry instructor at Coppice College for eighteen years, brought all this into a more concrete light through her reflectively iterative efforts to assess, gauge, and support students' readiness for online courses. Initially, like everyone else, she reactively strove to support all students in her online courses, but she soon realized that many students were not ready for online learning and that their sole reason for enrolling in online courses was out of convenience given their busy schedules—a legitimate but not fully informed *want*, given the many additional demands for being successful in remote learning. While respecting what many students *want*, especially those with full plates working and studying, Michelle was compelled to proactively bring clarity and depth to what students would *need* to succeed academically, online or not. So she started to reach out to students to give them clear guidelines on what needed to be in place for students to succeed in her online chemistry class, including time commitment, homework, math skills, and other course options: "But then giving them [other options], because we offer the hybrid and the face-to-face, and saying, 'Please use one of these courses if this isn't going to work for you.' Give them time to rearrange their schedule." In doing so, Michelle was offering her students the opportunity to assess whether the course would be a fit for them, as well as reflect on their learning styles, study skills, and scheduling needs. A compassionate instructor, Michelle was grappling with whether her communication with students this way was "harsh," as she was not immediately accepting students based on what they wanted. But in fact, students replied and thanked her for laying out these things for the first time ever and for caring about their success in the class.

Michelle's example illuminates an innovative direction toward better assessment and preparation for community and technical college students to thrive academically in online classes by revealing what is often hidden knowledge to them. Especially by engaging students with thoughtful questions and laying out clear expectations, she helped them reflect on their current learning styles and areas of study skills development in the context of scheduling and other important life circumstances. Acting with the kindness of clarity and some tough love, Michelle did the less popular thing on the front end, even in her own initial view. Yet her approach shines a light on a possible system of genuine compassion—largely nonexistent at this time—that sets up students for success on the front end so they can reconcile what they want with what they need to thrive in their education.

The faculty I interviewed, whether highlighted in this chapter or elsewhere, all thoughtfully changed or innovated one or more aspects of their teaching toward more inclusive and equitable student access, experiences, and outcomes, with compassion and grace forming the main underlying texture. All the issues they grappled with and the problems they strove to resolve are incredibly complex and delicate. Often, their choices and efforts require deep reflexivity, recalibration, and vulnerability to navigate. It is a developmental space that needs much support and community to learn and unlearn the craft of teaching. And in truth, many faculty shared experiences of remarkable growth and learning. Pandemic or not, compassion—anchored in equity, affirmation, clarity, and transparency—must remain at the forefront of how we engage with teaching and learning so that we do not dilute, but rather strengthen education to elevate students on their college and life journeys.

## QUESTIONS FOR REFLECTION

- How has the concept of flexibility, which became essential during the pandemic, shaped or reshaped faculty's approaches to teaching and learning?
- How do faculty navigate the tension between traditional expectations of rigor and the implementation of compassionate and inclusive teaching practices?
- How can faculty actively involve students in co-creating curricula and learning experiences to foster a sense of ownership and empowerment?
- When students appear to be struggling in online courses, how can educators initiate meaningful conversations to explore alternative modes or ways of learning that better suit their needs?
- How can instructors clearly communicate expectations, procedures, and supports for students considering enrollment in online classes?
- What policies or professional development can motivate and support faculty accustomed to traditional teaching methods to think outside the box and try new approaches?

- What are some of the potential barriers and challenges in implementing asset-based pedagogies and trauma-informed approaches, and how to address these issues?
- What are the long-term effects of asset-based pedagogies and trauma-informed approaches on student educational aspirations, progress, attainment, and overall well-being?

# 3

## Unclutter and Holisticize
## Student Support

*Thankfully, due to COVID, we opened up a lot of possibilities and we stopped doing a lot of things that amounted to barriers.*

—JEREMY, INSTRUCTOR AND ACADEMIC INTERVENTION ADVISOR,
RIDGELINE TECHNICAL COLLEGE

"HOW DO STUDENTS experience Central State College?" is a question underscored in numerous documents describing the strategic directions of the college. I learned about it through my multiple conversations with David. Having just assumed a new role as provost at the college, and with a background in teaching and student services, David's vision extends far beyond faculty work and into the range of support that students need in order to achieve educational success. It is a vision grounded in the question "How do students experience us?" and one that sets the stage for understanding the various innovative efforts highlighted in this chapter. These efforts not only aim to address the many complexities that go into the typical community college student experience but also strive to question the "typical" and remove some of those complexities, which should

57

not be there in the first place. Underlying these innovations is the fact that these educators have long been propelled by a new vision that delivers the necessary support for students to succeed, especially those from minoritized groups. For many, the pandemic offered a context to cast that vision in a more concrete light.

Chua, an academic advisor at Keystone College for eight years and now also a coordinator for community engagement, was both challenged and motivated by the pandemic to render student support differently. A Hmong woman, Chua experienced lots of emotions arising from myriad challenging personal contexts: being a mom of two kids with their school disrupted, helping take care of her father-in-law with underlying medical conditions, and grappling with racial injustices amplified at the time that were especially personal for Chua. She said, "I have never seen so much hate towards Asians. And I think that was just part of [me] being so young when you think of that. As before the pandemic, we already have all these racial pieces coming into play. And so now, we have this fear." On top of these personal challenges, Chua's work has also "changed dramatically." By that, she wasn't just talking about the multifold load as an advisor—both her official duties and her volunteer service role as an advisor to the Asian American Student Association at the college; Chua was also referring to the 180-degree turn in her perspective that allowed her and other advisors to maintain connections with students at a deeper and broader level. While she had had students' phone numbers and had some students as Facebook friends before the pandemic, she didn't believe she *should*. But now she tapped fully into these channels of communication to ensure her students were OK: "So, when it's times like this, you're very thankful that you have them as a [Facebook] friend. You can connect with them, right? So that has some advantage and that has really helped us really stay connected to our students. It's like, you know, the ability to adapt, to be quick."

Chua's shift came from her own challenges as described earlier. Rather than letting them consume all her energy, these challenges made it that much clearer to her that many students were struggling in much graver ways: "And so, where I know that my privilege comes from is that because I have the resources and the means, I was able to adapt quickly and pivot quickly. That's not the case for everyone here, right? So, for students and families, they might not have internet access, they don't have the technology access, they don't have transportation. I mean you're now talking about a whole lot of issues that come into play here."

Similar to the instructors I highlighted in chapter 2, how Chua and many educators in student support roles experienced the pandemic challenges brought them even closer to the realities of their students' lives. For as long as community colleges existed, the default model for students to gain support has been to sift through a simultaneously flexible and obscuring system on their own, all against a full slate of life contexts and obligations.[1] With the pandemic stripping away access and resources both inside and outside the college, the adverse impacts rapidly bled into education, employment, and society at large to affect the broader community in which students live, work, and learn. As a result, we end up with an already convoluted student support system that is further weakened. And the most vulnerable groups of students are simply not coming back.[2] Reflecting on this, Chua and her colleagues were deeply worried about current support approaches falling short: "And no matter what you say or do, students are not coming back. It is the mental health piece. The folks that are losing their loved ones to pandemic. Like, all we can do is to be available to be in this space to say hey, let's still connect, let's stay in touch with the hope that you'll come back."

While the challenges facing student support services are dire and daunting for these larger interlacing issues, my participants adopted innumerable small or big approaches to keeping students supported and engaged. These sometimes ingenious, sometimes imperfect, and always generative efforts extended beyond, while still touching upon, the classroom context. Although what I share here spans all stakeholder groups, this chapter is particularly driven by and devoted to those whose primary role involves student support, including those in direct advising roles. Their work is easily the most complex and challenging, and yet the most underappreciated, exactly because of the complexities and challenges involved, often owing to an untenable advising load.[3] Like their faculty counterparts, these staff members in various direct or indirect student support roles were challenged by and responded to the pandemic through new ways of helping students. Their stories are undergirded by a dual theme of holisticizing and uncluttering.

## HOLISTICIZING STUDENT SUPPORT TO HONOR THE WHOLE

By "holisticizing," I mean that the most prominent innovations are anchored within support and advising staff's attentiveness to a holistic set of challenges that compound to affect the most vulnerable student groups. The most immediate and telling of these challenges is finances. This need is easy to understand. Right at the beginning of the pandemic, there were national efforts like the Coronavirus Aid, Relief, and Economic Security (CARES) Act, which the US Congress passed to provide speedy funds right to the individuals negatively affected by COVID-19. A portion of this money was placed into the Higher Education Emergency Relief Fund so that institutions could distribute emergency grants and scholarships to students grappling with financial challenges.[4] The funds were intended to assist with food, housing, course materials, health care, child care, and technology, among other eligible areas.

One of the immediate things my participants highlighted was precisely the money made available to students. But how the money flows through the chain of divisions, units, and offices to reach and benefit students is a less straightforward issue. Having served as a student services professional for almost two decades, and currently as dean of student access and success, Reggie is determined not to accept the status quo. He was overseeing an emergency grant program in the financial aid office at Keystone College, as well as the Scholars Promise Program. Reggie always tells his staff, "It is not the student's responsibility to understand our processes. It is our responsibility to teach the student what our processes are and support them through them."

To realize that vision, Reggie was already leading the development of a virtual advising pilot that enabled financial aid staff to connect with students online. It was an innovation that tackled at least two key issues in financial aid advising. First, financial aid is notoriously difficult to apply for, as the necessary information changes and gets increasingly complex each year.[5] Add in the fact that many of the counselors are academic advisors who are not always equipped with all the information.[6] This initiative was meant to help demystify the process and provide direct guidance.

Second, financial aid advisors are in short supply in community and technical colleges, especially in rural settings.[7] This new initiative was intended to serve the regional campuses, several located in more rural areas. The college did not have enough staff for each of the campuses, which prompted Reggie to think of ways to creatively support students' financial needs, essentially on demand. Once the pandemic hit, this initiative was fast-tracked into action to connect students with the services they needed. Reggie said, "So, we were moving on in the process to where we were developing it. When the pandemic hit, it was like, OK, we got to turn it on, because we don't have time to push it out a couple more months. This is a necessity, or a need of our students. So it was that whole aspect of how do we serve our students?"

Not only did Reggie and his team accelerate their virtual advising project, but he also started to realize that, in the world of financial aid, the flexibilities that have been provided were not fully utilized. So he set his mind toward simplifying the process. Reggie approached this change from a holistic view of the student experience and struggles:

> We need to allow innocent students to make mistakes and just trust that is going to go through just perfectly fine. I think this pandemic has unveiled many of the challenges that our students have been facing over the years that we had a blind eye to. As far as the inequity of different things, access to resources, access to digital equity, even

the level of basic needs that students need in order to be successful while attending our institutions. All that has now been unveiled, and we now have to respond. We have a responsibility to respond in order to be able to start our students and make sure that they are covered in a holistic aspect of it, and not just an academic mindset.

Certainly, there is a holistic aspect to the student experience that affects their academics, and the student support educators came up with innovative approaches to address a wide range of issues, such as limited access to technology, basic needs insecurity, and mental health difficulties. To name just a few from the countless examples reflected in news articles and institutional communications, some colleges launched free technology access programs for students to request laptops, hot spots, and everything else that is required for students enrolled in credit-bearing courses. When it came to basic needs, at Ridgeline Technical College, for example, new positions were established to provide targeted support, like a basic needs resource navigator. Students can put in requests, and a staff member will help connect them to the necessary resources and supports. As for mental health, multiple institutions implemented a suite of programming, such as new classes with a focus on well-being and mental health and free online therapy. These are just a few of the rich volume of inspiring efforts to support the whole student on multiple levels.

There also emerged a holistic take on supporting various student transitions through their academic journeys during challenging times. A case in point is Asia, a student support advisor at Keystone College who serves as an all-around resource for students. He described how his biggest concerns were about how to help the most vulnerable, especially returning adults, students with disabilities, and nontraditional age students, navigate the college landscape and figure out how to be willing to receive assistance: "It's not a reflection of a character; it's just a barrier to education that they have lived with, and they have been successful and living with it, but we can make their time here more effective and efficient." For Asia, the pandemic only heightened the familiar challenges these students faced, making it even more urgent that he support them more creatively and proactively so they would not experience permanent consequences: "The goal of my position is to make it an easier transition and to be proactive in anything that may come up, and life-changing, especially during the pandemic. That students can utilize our resources, so they don't have a financial burden, or it doesn't impact their GPA or cause any irreparable academic damages to their record in the future."

Asia's vision and approaches, grounded in supporting the whole person, resonate with so many other educators working in similar capacities, such as Anthony, executive director of student services at Parkfield Technical College, who oversees all the functions that would be categorized under student services or student affairs: recruitment, admissions, the registrar, financial aid, advising, student engagement, counseling services, and career services. Like Asia, Anthony is highly attuned to these areas in relation to students' goals, needs, life contexts, and challenges: "My students, most of them have no intention of leaving this area. They have family commitments. They have work commitments. They have reasons that they're staying here. You have to be immersed in who your student population is, what their needs are, what their makeup is, what their obstacles are. And it's not just about creating a fair playing field. It's about immersing yourself in those individual needs and characteristics of your whole population." To better serve this population, Anthony teamed up with faculty, advisors, admissions, the registrar, and others to establish a new task force called the "student experience group" to holistically support student progress and examine the challenges that may interfere with it.

## UNCLUTTERING STUDENT SUPPORT FOR EQUITY

Parallel to holisticizing is "uncluttering"—meaning that many student support participants described their most innovative practices as actually doing away with long-standing structures or practices that have been in the way of students making progress. "Thankfully, due to COVID, we opened up a lot of possibilities and we stopped doing a lot of things that amounted to barriers," said Jeremy, an instructor and academic intervention advisor, in response to my question about innovative things to highlight; he was citing their High School Equivalency Diploma (HSED) program as a key innovation. His colleague, Paddy, coordinator for reentry education services, couldn't have agreed more. Jeremy and Paddy, both with experience teaching in prisons and working with justice-involved individuals, serve in numerous student support capacities for the HSED program at Ridgeline Technical College.[8] They teach and advise; they support students transitioning to a college environment; help them navigate services and resources; and counsel them on continuing education and completing their general education development (GED) credentials. I first read about their work in several newspapers. When I reached out to Paddy and Jeremy about an interview, they requested to be interviewed as a team, as that's what they've always been.

As a team, they shared their *why*. Early in the conversation, Paddy described how his experience with a sixty-two-year-old woman looking to complete her GED shaped his approaches to student support—removing as many barriers as possible so as to make the impossible possible. In this case, Paddy worked with an older adult who wanted to complete her GED but never thought it was possible because, rightfully, she was aware of the typically cumbersome and excessive tests and requirements. So she was only casually inquiring into some general information about the college when this topic came up. But to Paddy, there was nothing casual about it. He went above and beyond to look into her record—high school credits and employment history, making everything she'd done and studied count, and then he simplified the option to taking a civics test, "literally the easiest one." When she realized she now had a real option—a most simple, straightforward option—she started to cry instantly. Paddy recalled, "And I'm like, oh no, 'This is good as you know, this is really good. This is a good thing,' and she's just like, 'No, no,

I know it is. I just I never thought I'd be able—I never thought I'd be able to do this. I thought I was gonna die without like having my HSED. My son's gonna be so proud of me. He also is now interested in completing his HSED, and now knowing about Mom.'" Just like that, Paddy helped clear the way to turn what appeared out of reach into a tangible reality.

Being able to identify the roadblocks and remove them for students is part of their *why*, and the story of the sixty-two-year-old woman is not just one anecdote. Jeremy described how, at a larger scale, innovations following that spirit of removing barriers were burgeoning in their HSED program: "So real specifically, when Paddy was talking about that one civics test for that sixty-two-year-old person, that really became an option. That became an option in part due to COVID, because we started to look holistically at all the work that students had been doing leading up to the point of enrollment." He went on to explain how the dominant models entail an excessive amount of work without necessarily honoring what students had already done or known: "Before then, like when I first started, students had two choices to complete their High School Equivalency Diploma. They had to do five tests, or they had to do the HSED program in full, which was five units plus some tests, plus a portfolio."

In retrospect, both Paddy and Jeremy felt that COVID-19 helped actualize a shared vision to resolve a long-standing shared issue of concern, shifting from individual efforts to changes in policy and structures. In Jeremy's words:

> COVID really pushed us toward looking, in total, at what students had accomplished at that point and merging—for example, high school work, standardized test scores, portfolios, work experiences, all this stuff—so that was a big one. We also, at that time, stopped doing Accuplacer testing to place people in college courses. We got rid of our admissions fees, which up until that point had just been for a particular segment of our student population. In some cases, we stopped

doing high school diploma verification. We just took students' word for [it], instead of requiring them to submit paperwork.

Paddy and Jeremy joined their numerous counterparts in uncluttering student experiences. The HSED is just one telling example of the larger change and innovation to various student support efforts guided by the principle of confronting and removing long-existing barriers. Pre-pandemic, the kinds of structures or practices that Jeremy, Paddy, and others described, like admissions fees, placement tests, cumbersome application processes for awards, and so on, were barely questioned despite the lack of practical and empirical backing for their rigor. Since the pandemic, though, they have been brought under much deeper scrutiny by practitioners at a time when upholding practices that add to the burden of students—especially those less privileged—became untenable.

Irene, the associate dean who oversees the learner support and transition division and the Learning Center—what she calls the "hub and the heart of learning" at Ridgeline Technical College, described how the pandemic amplified barriers for the student populations that she was most concerned about: those reentering college, refugee learners, and justice-involved students; and how this concern introduced a clear shift in her and her team's mindset toward uncluttering student experiences for those most inequitably affected: "We try not to move at the pace of privilege; we try to move at the pace of the needs of the students, moving at the state of urgency versus catering to those who need to be comfortable." Sonya, vice president of administration at Keystone College, similarly highlighted changes to encourage breaking down barriers for various student groups, like those with children: "One in four community college students is a parent and not having access to consistent quality care is a huge stressor in their lives. That really detracts from them participating in their education, so that's been a big project that we've been working on."

Harnessing the rich examples and insights across myriad domains of student experiences, three themes converged, each speaking to an essential facet of how students experience college: *access*, *readiness*, and *navigation*, as exemplified by changes that removed costly requirements and brought transparency to courses, programs, and resources; revisited admissions processes; and smoothened policies and procedures to enhance advising and make it easier for students to get through college, all of which I discuss next.

## Broadening Access

The very first critical area in need of uncluttering is access at a deeper level. Many educators I interviewed contended with new ways of rendering student support out of a common concern that, while students are able to get through the door, they are quickly confronted with a slew of obstacles that impede their access to courses, programs, and resources. Precious, a Black woman and dean of health sciences at Afton Community College, has long grappled with this issue, having worked with low-income students for decades. She pinpointed the irony that programs like hers, allied health and nursing, are meant to provide economic mobility for students from low-income families, and yet persistent financial barriers made access to such programs costly and prohibitive to these very students. She described the range of standardized tests students had to take, with the expectation that they were to pick up the growing tab. And this only ended up with the programs serving students from more affluent backgrounds, causing deep equity concerns. Precious added, "So you bring them all in, and then you put the roadblock up. But you cannot get in these programs that are going to remove you from that lower socioeconomic environment. You know all these things they were asking them to do [taking standardized tests] was a cost to the students. So, you know the caliber [of] students we were getting—those whose parents could afford to do all these things." As a result, Precious led a large effort to change the college's admissions and program entry requirements, part of which resulted in the removal of costly requirements, leading to greater, more equitable access to her programs without a hefty price tag attached.

A new way to extend and deepen access also means being more intentional about what resources are shrouded in the current structures, or even withheld from minoritized students who could benefit, and bringing those resources into a clearer light. Asia emphasized resources specific to the Department of Vocational Rehabilitation (DVR) as a key example: "What I've seen, just my personal experience, and observations, that for families, or people of color, that there are gatekeepers potentially to DVR as a resource. That's open to anyone, but that information will not be shared, because someone may believe this particular individual does not have the capacity to go to higher education or enter the workforce. So that information is withheld from the students and their loved ones." With the pandemic pushing Asia to confront his own long-standing concern about resources and information not made transparent to students, he was determined to change the default model of having students ask for what they need. Asia would clearly lay out all the resources for students so they would have clear access to all the options and information to make decisions.

Plus, it wasn't just about sharing all the information; it was about sharing it in a timely manner so that students could assess their individual circumstances and understand the different outcomes of potential decisions, like withdrawing from classes and its potential consequences on financial aid. He would problem-solve with students to make sure that all resources and options were on the table to avoid missteps or penalties. Instead of reinforcing inequitable access to information and resources for students, Asia turned the conversation and action to, "Here's the resources, do with it what you may."

## Affirming Readiness

Student readiness is another policy area where some major uncluttering needs to occur. Often, even within open access institutions such as community and technical colleges, placement tests and rigid admissions requirements for high-demand programs act as barriers to minoritized students accessing educational opportunities by preventing them from enrolling in their desired courses and programs, or even discouraging them from attending college altogether.[9] Back to Precious and the larger reform she led to change the college's admissions process—a feat driven by her deep concerns about equity: "I've always thought that the admission processes for health programs were not fair. They were not fair. They were not equitable." She dug into the policies and student data, challenging the long-established testing requirements and whether and how the tests truly gauged who would be the "best" or "successful" students:

> They could not show me how making a sixty-eight on a TEAS [Test of Essential Academic Skills] test guaranteed success. But what they did show me was GPA [grade point average] was important. Guess what the new process is now? GPA. I'm only looking at the students' GPA. We noticed that the students who had taken biology before they got into the program were more successful. So we're gonna get out of their way. Now the students have to complete a bio class and have a 2.8 GPA, because we noticed 2.8 was that benchmark and they were still doing well.

While GPA isn't everything, it moves further toward honoring students' holistic readiness and removing placement tests that are not that valid, are costly, and act as barriers to instead of boosters of both access and success. Precious's example demonstrates that reevaluating traditional approaches to program entry, such as placement testing or other assessments, is essential to helping a more diverse student population to achieve their educational and occupational goals.

## Smoothening Navigation

With the historical cafeteria-style advising, academic policies and support structures can sometimes feel like a maze to navigate.[10] Ironically, it is not something that all my participants recognized before the pandemic, being on the "provider" end for so long. But many of them do now. In response, they came up with new solutions that unclutter the

student experience to ensure a more holistic and easier college navigation process. Some of this happened at the structural level. For instance,
Reggie recounted numerous existing documentation policies and procedures around transcripts, forms, and other documents, which were predominantly paper-based: "There were some things that were built into
regulations and policy that required a physical signature. So a student
couldn't access a form online and sign it, or scan and send it to us. We
had to actually have the physical wet signature, which kind of prompted
a wave of other things to say, we need to make some changes in order to
really adjust, to be able to support our students." Reggie explained how
these approaches only amounted to barriers for students making their
way through college, especially during the pandemic: "We're adding to
the complexity of what they're experiencing, and we have to remove
things in order to make sure that playing field is level." This realization
accelerated growing efforts to clear away long-established regulations
and requirements that were not serving students well, making a switch
from paper-based documentation to electronic.

Perhaps more frequently and more readily, uncluttering how students
navigate college happens at the individual level, often within advising contexts. Kevin, an academic advisor at Midwest Technical College,
spoke of "being a thought partner with students to identify the clutter
that could get in the way." The clutter could mean the influx of sometimes conflicting information that students try to reconcile in making
their academic choices and decisions; so he started implementing regular pauses during advising meetings to check students' understanding
of the information and relevant steps, and then correcting or clarifying
as they go. "Clutter" could also refer to the complexities arising from all
the procedures entailed in the typical convoluted process toward transfer; so he developed a new transfer intent form to simplify the process
and related information, working in cross-functional teams to bring all
pieces and parties on the same page, literally. Kevin views advising as
a humanizing relationship-building process that empowers students to

navigate college in a clear, informed way. For Kevin, "empowerment is the ultimate prize" that comes out of this uncluttered experience.

Uncluttering student experiences requires hard, reflective work that interrogates the roots—where the need to unclutter came from in the first place—resides. As Reggie described, "it used to be, it still exists in the financial aid land, but sometimes we take our own personal beliefs and thoughts and backgrounds and infuse that on the people that we're serving because we've experienced it, or we don't trust it." Often, the clutter that Reggie referred to resides in deeply ingrained mindsets, encompassing structures and processes rooted in whiteness. As a result, this type of clutter inhibits true progress and perpetuates inequities in students' experiences. Although in some cases, uncluttering is motivated by the need to manage and survive, distinct from faculty participants, the support and advising staff I interviewed, white and nonwhite, showed a compelling grappling with whiteness in their practice of providing student support at community and technical colleges. These educators reflected on how whiteness permeated various college and course processes that they now learned to unclutter. Take Jeremy as an example. Through some hard, difficult reflection, he came to recognize "all the implicit ways that a white supremacist culture shows up, like the need for paperwork, and intake forms, and precise scheduling, and linear and abstract thinking over the concrete value." These tough but valuable awakenings resulted in a shift for Jeremy, "putting the onus for change on me, so that we can adjust and serve people who have not been served by educational systems and employment systems." Digging into and confronting the root of clutter, including deeply steeped whiteness, play a key role in stripping away obstacles to student supports and paths.

In tandem with this reckoning with whiteness is the rising "student-ready" ethos. Ali, vice president of learning at Midtown College, described this shift in mindset: "[In our past practices], we always ask if the students are college ready. Are you ready? We tested them, you're not ready, go back. We can't accept you, we can't admit you, and so on and so forth. We reversed that question, and we asked: Are we 'student-ready'? Meaning to say any individual student that came to our college deserved education, are we ready for our students? And if they're not ready because of a test, what can we do to get them ready?" As detailed earlier in the chapter, participants shared many examples where they changed their own practices at the individual level to fully meet student needs. More important, though, being student-ready involves dismantling some of the most obstructive institutional policies and structures that do not actually serve students, as illuminated in the examples of Jeremy, Paddy, and Precious removing admissions fees or placement tests to improve access to programs that students would otherwise be shut out of. All told, these educators are determined to put the onus for change on themselves. Seeing the impact reflected in a much smoother, uncluttered student experience accessing and benefiting from the intended support compels these stakeholders to reimagine an equity-centered student support and services model for the future.

As we come to the end of this chapter, I would like to highlight a key innovation: the Student Resource Center (SRC) developed by Boricua and his team. As you may recall from the introduction to this book, Boricua expressed a keen concern about the uneven access that students had to support services. Rather than relying on individual student support staff, he saw this as a broader institutional issue that required reforming workflows, processes, and structures. His vision comes as no surprise, as he is known for his "innovation, an agile mindset, and a dedication to moving the institution forward," according to his colleagues quoted in an institutional news article. He started small and yet extensive by transforming various spaces at the college into workstations where staff could connect with students and guide them to the supports that they needed: "With two or three staff per day, and any student coming through our door, whether they're connecting with us through our website, through chat, whether they were walking through the door, we would then be able to connect them with the type of support that they were searching." The workstations had dual monitors, which enabled both the students and employees to view and interact with shared information. They also provided keyboards and mice for real-time input from students. With this approach, Boricua and his team were able to catch any student coming through the door, literally handing all students access to supports and resources, even the most unlikely ones to seek help proactively.

Over the course of two years, Boricua and his team expanded, redesigned, and repurposed various spaces on campus to create the SRC. In 2022, coinciding with Boricua becoming the first male Latinx vice president and chief student services officer at Afton Community College, the SRC was unveiled. The center contains a library, bookstore, food pantry, financial aid advising, course advising, admissions, registration, and community connections. It is a comprehensive infrastructure that delivers access to the full spectrum of student support services. From the video he proudly shared with me, the space is bright and inviting, with clear signs and directions for all supports and services. Students literally have direct access to everything.

When asked how it was all made possible, Boricua attributed this feat to collaboration through inquiry and a common commitment. He brought all units on board by recognizing their expertise and asking for their input, spanning executive and midlevel leadership, directors, security, information technology (IT) services, and advisors, among others. He asked questions like, "How do you see this happening? What I would do is this, but I'm not coming to your area telling you this is what it's going to be. Let me share with you my thoughts on what I believe needs to happen, and you are the specialist. This is your area of expertise and proficiency. How could you support the SRC if this is how we're operating?" By doing so, he built authentic commitment from all areas of the college.

Simply put, the SRC is a shining example of educational innovation in community and technical colleges, made possible by a shared vision and collective effort leading to a transformed support system that serves students during and beyond crises. It is guided by a holistic student support vision and uncluttering many of the unnecessary structures and processes. It is a true one-stop shop, with "students receiving what they need, when they need it," Boricua said.

*How do students experience us?* In different shapes and forms, this question has become the new overarching framework that has guided the numerous changes and adaptations by the educators in this book. On the surface level, it reads similar to the question that higher education practitioners and researchers ask perennially: *What are the students' experiences?* But fundamentally, these two questions are different. *How do students experience us?* is a question that implores us, the educators, to carry the onus of making possible a holistic and uncluttered student experience. It implies that we look within ourselves and our policies, structures, processes, practices, and mindsets for answers to resolve the challenges and barriers in student experiences that seem forever difficult to solve. As illuminated by the educators in this chapter, this shift in perspective brings clarity, direction, and feasibility, as it requires identifying things that they can actually do. As challenging as this work continues to be, it's worth every small or big step forward so that all there is to transpire on the student end feels smooth and seamless; it is not effortless, as students still have to do their own hard work, but it's an experience defined by hopefulness toward a clear *so-what*.

## QUESTIONS FOR REFLECTION

- How does the integration of technology, digital platforms, and online resources affect the accessibility and equity of student support services?
- What approaches and strategies are helpful for empowering students and promoting their agency and self-advocacy within the support system?

- What current policies and structures pose the biggest barriers to equitable student access to resources, supports, courses, or programs?
- What policy changes are needed to enhance the communication of policies and procedures around course and program requirements?
- What strategies can be implemented to improve communication and collaboration among student support professionals?
- How can policy makers and education leaders bring together the expertise of multiple service and support units toward developing holistic and equitable student support systems?
- How can community and technical colleges streamline student support systems to achieve a more holistic and coordinated experience for students?

# 4

## Reflectively Engage Data and Institutional Research

*If an institution is really operating in the way that I think it should,*
*the IR [institutional research] folks should really be the start of some of the*
*innovation or changes happening at the institution.*

—JILL, ENROLLMENT MANAGEMENT ANALYST, KEYSTONE COLLEGE

JILL'S HEART WAS "filled with happiness and gratitude" when describing
how her analysis comparing pre-pandemic and during-pandemic completion rates in online classes was used to prioritize interventions and
instructional modes at Keystone College. Having spent eleven years in
several roles across academic advising and institutional research (IR) at
the college, Jill is currently an enrollment management analyst working
with various institutional data to help with "all things academic affairs."
Jill firmly believes in the power of using sound data to drive change, but
she admitted that this is rare in decision-making about interventions
in higher education. At her own college, the default model used to be,
"We're going to intervene [regardless], and maybe if the data lines are
just right, we will use it." Still, Jill routinely produces reports based on

programmatic and institutional data, hoping that ultimately more of her colleagues will see what she sees as the million-dollar question: "How can we use data in academic affairs to change our services or to improve our practices?"

Consumed by that same question, Jill acted with an even more heightened sense of urgency during the pandemic because of "how timely everything is, and how often you need to redo things." She approached her online course completion analysis by disaggregating the data based on a set of student backgrounds such as age, gender, and race, and she found that racially underrepresented students had significantly lower online course completion rates during the height of the pandemic. The response from leadership and faculty to Jill's report was not one that she was used to pre-pandemic: "People cared about this in a way that I didn't expect. This was one of those [situations] where I'm gonna send it out and see if people care. But we got a list of courses and programs from this that were priorities for intervention, and it was one of those 'data for practice' situations and I was super pleased with it." Jill later explained how, based on the data, college leadership developed interventions and allocated resources aimed at closing racial equity gaps where the course completion rates of students of color were down: "I'm really happy with how some of that has turned out. Instead of it just being data, we used that as one of the factors, along with many other factors. We did more intentional intervening because of what the data said. That's very cool."

Both Jill's delight and surprise were well founded. Although data-driven decision-making has been a sounding horn in higher education since forever, it was not until recent years that equity-minded use of data began to gain traction with practitioners.[1] The pandemic context changed both how various stakeholders engage data and the speed at which they use the data for innovation and intervention. As illustrated in Jill's example, "Things change so much more quickly than they used to, whether or not this is even month to month, which never used to matter in our data. It super matters how timely things are now in a way that didn't used to be true." Jill embraced this shift that feels like a much-awaited answer to her long-standing prayer: "If an institution is really operating in the way that I think it should, the IR folks should really be the start of some of the innovation or changes happening at the institution."

I am arriving at this chapter with a soft spot in my heart, having shared, albeit briefly, a professional identity as an institutional researcher. Jill's sentiment also rings true with the distinct group of institutional researchers I interviewed—a highly important yet underaddressed stakeholder group in the higher education literature. They perform some of the most high-stakes, intricate data work within every piece of the fabric of institutional operation, and yet often remain invisible to their colleagues and within the education research discourse. Still, these professionals and the field in which they practice—broadly described as institutional research—have been in place for as long as any other institutional stakeholder group at community and technical colleges. On a personal level and in full transparency, having traversed the IR field, I have long held a deep respect for and affinity with the IR professionals in any community and technical college partnership that I have built as a university-based researcher. Over the course of the past thirteen years, I have collaborated with and established a lasting rapport with some of the most extraordinary IR professionals and leaders, some of whom I feature in this chapter. My own professional experiences, alongside these carefully cultivated relationships with IR colleagues prior to this research, lend depth and authenticity to my understanding of these individuals' engagement in the changes, challenges, and rewards of the crucial work that they carry out.

What Jill touched upon resonates with the rest of the IR professionals I interviewed—the value they saw in data and IR and the potential equity solutions that lie within the data. In fact, these appeared to be long-held values and beliefs among the IR professionals I interviewed, and yet disappointingly, these values and beliefs were more often a vision than a reality, restricted by institutional politics, bureaucracies, trust issues, and above all, resistance to the use of evidence. As a result, institutional researchers' roles are typically constrained and construed as data stewards for reporting compliance and occasional institutional surveys, with limited potential for using those data for decision-making in real time. These difficulties are further complicated and compounded at smaller community and technical colleges, where IR capacity is stretched even thinner, as it is not rare to have only one person carrying out this role, either full time or split up with other roles. But as Jill alluded to, the catalyzing waves of the pandemic's impacts changed how IR professionals and other stakeholders engage data in supporting proliferating new efforts, which are often layered with glaring equity gaps further exposed by the pandemic.

Throughout the rest of this chapter, I further unpack IR professionals' experiences in generating data and supporting their use to guide decisions and innovative solutions during the pandemic. With an unapologetic focus on IR, I also integrate other stakeholders' perspectives and experiences in relation to using data for equity-driven change. Ultimately, these stories reinforce the significance of engaging data reflectively to inform everything going on at all levels of the institution, especially when it comes to serving students, which represents the very core of the institutional mission.

## "OUR STUDENTS ARE NOT JUST STATISTICS": HUMANIZING DATA AND INTERPRETATION

A few short months into the pandemic, institutional researchers saw a sharp increase in the requests from faculty, leaders, and staff for various student data. This booming interest has led to steady growth in the scope and complexity of the data work needed to be done. However, IR professionals and others engaging data strive to maintain their focus by infusing humanity into the data and related interpretations. In the words of Boricua, "When you look at data, we're not just looking at numbers. Those numbers represent people. Those numbers are your constituents, your stakeholders. Those numbers are individuals who you don't know what they have sacrificed to be in that place and at that moment. If we can start to humanize data, maybe it can help motivate us to transform how we do our work."

The possible human experiences, good or bad, behind the data are also the lens through which many IR professionals engage right away when looking at data. Victoria, director of institutional research at Keystone College, shared some of the immediate new efforts she and her team took up at the onset of the pandemic: "One of the very first few things was, we had to pivot as a college and look all the students up. What are they doing? What do they need? So those are some of the initiatives that vice president of student services did. We were involved in that to summarize some of the data there, and some of the findings [to inform]." This vantage point extends far beyond merely utilizing data as performance metrics; rather, it emphasizes leveraging data to prioritize the well-being of students as human beings first and foremost. Something extraordinary, according to Victoria, was her college's use of data and IR expertise to guide the sudden pivot in March 2020 in real time: "How can we transition our in-person classes to online and well, students who have no technology right off the bat are at a disadvantage because they have no technology to actually be able to even do their classes. It's also about Wi-Fi and things like that. So those were some of the different types of research that we were involved with our IT department, like where should we, or who should we partner with, to help our students be able to access Wi-Fi?" As a result, this data gathering and collaboration helped Keystone College in its efforts to support students in all these ways to alleviate concerns about access, enrollment, and resources during the transition to remote learning.[2] Generating data to help identify and enact this type of change drives Victoria's work. As a first-generation college student from a Hmong refugee family, Victoria started her two-decades-long IR career at the college as a research specialist and moved through all the essential roles and stages of the IR field to land at her current position as director of IR. There has always been a sense of mission that grounds her within the IR work: "Looking back, that service component in IR—helping people— has always been something that I considered to be a mission-critical thing for me."

The same commitment and urgency around using data to guide student support resonate with Sue, who works at Midtown College. Having been in IR at the college for eighteen years and in her director of IR role for the past nine, Sue has been unflagging in her efforts and integrity to make a space for IR at the table when it comes to important decisions affecting students, even if it means adding more work to her plate. For Sue, it's all about having the data at hand at the onset to prevent people from going down the wrong path—data *uninformed*—only to not serve students as intended. The pandemic brought to fuller light the significance and impact of her long-standing approaches that put data front and center. Sue shared with me that there were many concurrent efforts occurring at Midtown College, all meant to generate holistic, equitable approaches to supporting students' academic progress, particularly tying academics to other areas of student supports and needs, like advising, financial aid, well-being, and more. As an example, she highlighted a regional equity initiative that the college joined, a core component of which was a student success platform that shares data and information across multiple units and users, including advisors, retention coaches, student success liaisons, faculty, and other staff. These users can access and share student records, notes, and information so that students receive proactive support from the necessary service or support area— rendering holistic, coordinated support so "students are not falling through the cracks." To pull off these complex and interconnected efforts, Sue was brought in to guide the development of a streamlined data process to ensure a consistent, accurate, and standardized flow of data not only across the various participating units within the college, but also other institutions they partnered with.

Across the colleges, there has also been a swift uptake to use data to guide instructional and scheduling changes burgeoning during the pandemic. While course scheduling and related student decisions frequently muddle academic progress through community and technical colleges, the pandemic unveiled unprecedented pivots and messiness that accentuated the urgency to address the enduring concern around often-unquestioned, arbitrary decisions about academic scheduling. Sonya, vice president of administration at Keystone College, among other leadership roles there for the past eight years, captured this urgency when she described the potential of analyzing the "enormous amount of data about students and their course-taking behaviors" to guide these instructional and scheduling changes: "One of the things that we're now very cognizant of is making sure that when we're sequencing classes, that we do not double, that we do not schedule two classes that somebody may need to graduate at the same time. Because then you obviously can't finish your degree."

It is not just about sequencing; modality and frequency also matter. Sonya recognized that course and scheduling options could put a kink in student progress, especially when specific program requirements must be met. The data shed crucial light on this issue, enabling the college to "be really thoughtful about not having students wait too long between those offerings." Moreover, Sonya described how institutional data were used to help the college optimize a mix of online and in-person sections for broader electives. This prompted a deeper level of reflection and data analysis that takes into account the complexities of students and their decision-making when choosing courses. The shift also involves moving away from course scheduling and modalities that solely prioritize instructors and their preferences without considering students' multifaceted needs. Sonya said, "So we incorporate that into our thinking and our planning as part of what we need to do. Think about course times and sequencing, and modality, as opposed to just modality. Before, it was more of an afterthought and more based around preferences like, I prefer to teach online or I'm gonna be in Japan for a semester, so I have to teach my classes remotely, or whatever it is." This reorientation toward data engagement tackles some of the old problems and paves the way for forward-oriented planning. It reflects the evolving complexities in course and instructional offerings while remaining deeply responsive to the multifaceted needs of students.

These and other examples all bring a humanistic light to what's often viewed as dry, objective data work. As Victoria put it, "A lot of time people who are in the data areas especially, they talk about data. But it's separated from students, and it may be because once people might say, that's just a statistic. *Our students are not just statistics.* They are actual, real-life, breathing students who are impacted by the different things that we do." Indeed, if critically engaging institutional data is truly meant to improve the lives and circumstances of the most marginalized students, the same humanity that grounds everything else in education must also be positioned front and center with regard to the data and related work that flow through the institutions that serve those students.

## USING DATA TO ILLUMINATE PATTERNS
## OF DISPARITIES AND INEQUITIES

Arguably starting from that place of care, my participants shared examples of new ways in which data are used for equity, often starting with how faculty and academic leaders engage enrollment and outcomes data in a different and new light. Lauren, vice president of academic affairs at Keystone College, described how, through a critical look at the data, the college was able to interrogate its initial efforts in deciding class modalities through a simplistic adoption of a priority system that "kept anything online that we could keep online." Looking more closely into student success data, she noticed large disparities based on the types of classes. In particular, classes that tended to enroll student populations facing more structural and contextual barriers were not serving these students well in the pandemic-induced online modality. Lauren reflected: "We need to get the ESL students back into the classroom because we're seeing student success and access issues. We need to get our developmental students in math and reading and writing back because we had some student success issues going there." On the other hand, less disadvantaged students tended to do well in online classes, and for these classes, keeping them online was less concerning, especially given issues of operational capacity and student demand for convenience during continuously intricate times. As Lauren described: "There are some programs like our Human Services program that actually, the student success and the access [had] increased. Our enrollment went up. They were doing better, so that program today is still fully online." She further shared that reflectively engaging with the student success data prompted questions like, "How do we need to be delivering this to students?" In their pursuit of answers to such questions, Lauren and others started with transforming their decision-making mindset from one that used to be a default to precedence and anecdotes to one involving the use of data with a heightened level of care for students that are not equitably served by certain modalities.

Lauren's example is telling, both about the ever-more-complex decision-making about course modalities—a massive, common issue that all institutions have been contending with since COVID-19 opened Pandora's box—and about how vital it is for colleges to engage high-quality data to guide related, often difficult decisions. Earlier, in chapter 2, I shared some examples of thoughtful approaches to online teaching, but what we grapple with here is a far bigger structural issue than the pedagogy. It's about who gets what types of education, who benefits, and who deals with unintended consequences. In the context of online education, minoritized students tend to get trapped and make little progress.[3] Further putting these students at a disadvantage are fewer academic supports, technical difficulties, and online learning not reducing costs to students.[4] Ultimately, online education tends to benefit students who are well prepared, well resourced, and predisposed to learning in a virtual environment, further widening equity gaps and pushing colleges to use their data to confront these challenges head-on as they restructure online options.

The inequities embedded within online education are further complicated by the pandemic, as it appeared to have opened far more possibilities than before. Many students themselves, regardless of their background, seem to desire online learning for its convenience and expediency. Yet, as I alluded to in chapter 2, these trends and aspirations could be part of a false narrative that online education is the great new equalizer and panacea. My IR participants were very wary about this perspective and spoke about the urgent need for gathering data to inform decisions. In the words of Sue, "We are very challenged right now in terms of how to support scheduling, in terms of what is the best delivery, because it's kind of all over the place. Then how do you decide which one to offer? I think I really feel like the academic division is very challenged; no matter how they offer it, there will always be students [who] say, 'Oh, I want the other way.' So we still have to figure out how to do it." Sue's IR team started to gather student survey data, but seeing that "the data responses are all over the place," Sue has been tapping her IR professional networks beyond her college for ideas and best practices. While the ultimate answer still seems out of immediate reach, the reflective ways in which Lauren, Sue, and others paused and resteered their thinking is refreshingly generative as we continue the difficult work of producing and using data thoughtfully for solving this complicated puzzle.

Underneath these burgeoning efforts to engage institutional data was an increasingly more critical and careful focus on racial differences. For the IR participants I interviewed, this attention and interest align with their long-standing desire to use data critically to enact change, as expressed in the sentiments of IR professionals whom I highlighted earlier in the chapter. Notably, Victoria never contemplated leaving IR, but not because she didn't enjoy "frontline" student services roles, or any other roles; to the contrary, she is all about centering students. But she saw something unique and vital in the IR field that best positions her to realize her student-centered, equity-guided vision: "If the data is not collected, then certain groups or certain entities will be systematically left out. From that equity perspective, unless we can give the data to the point where we can do some of those dissection and review in details if there's any differences and gaps and things like that, we're not going to be able to really improve equity for people."

This convergence sets the perfect stage for various stakeholders to engage with data that center students in equitable, humanizing ways. At Keystone College, Victoria's team is in the process of creating reports for faculty and staff to see how students of color experience various programs, course offerings, and campus locations. More important for Victoria is engaging faculty in a critical examination of their course data: "Does the fact that out of their classes, one out of two African American students are successful. Is that OK? And if they look at it over time, that pattern may carry, and is that OK? When you look at it, holistically, as a college, is that OK? So that's the pieces that we need to take a look at, because our world is changing. The demographics of our students are changing. We have students who are coming in with more barriers, economic and academic." Even at less racially diverse colleges, such as Meadowland Technical College, a rural, predominantly white college, IR director Janet acknowledged the institution's geographical contexts and racial composition without losing sight of how critical it is to ensure racially underrepresented students in the area "feel like we're a safe place to come and that they're welcome." She employed engagement and diversity survey data, "trying to get a sense of how welcome our students feel, not only how successful are they, but kind of what's going on, and are we serving these [racially underrepresented] populations well?"

This heightened focus on racial equity is against the backdrop of the larger diversity, equity, and inclusion (DEI) efforts that proliferated on many campuses during the pandemic. For instance, DEI efforts at Midtown College provided Sue with the opportunity to develop tools and resources for the institution to take a hard look at the data through a racial equity lens—such as a dashboard that not only provides aggregate collegewide data like course success rates, but also various ways to disaggregate the data based on race, ethnicity, gender, and many other factors. It opened many of her colleagues' eyes, Sue shared, adding that "we certainly see a big difference." For Sue, approaching her IR work from a racial equity perspective is imperative for supporting key college initiatives. Case in point: Sue's analysis of IR data was instrumental in launching the college's new program, where exploring students can apply as "undecided" and receive coaching and guidance toward a program of study when entering college. With her analytical eye toward the "root cause," Sue first identified big racial equity gaps in program completion rates between Black and white students and then found that the disparate program completion rates among students of color could be traced to a haphazard and uninformed program-selection process. With the support of these data, the development of the new program and option on the application form would "give opportunity to students as undecided and we will help them find their career passion, and then sign them up for the program that aligns. So then that's kind of helping to reduce the gap between students of color or first-generation students who tend not to have help from their family to select the career they might be interested or good at. So that's why we are helping on this one." Breaking down the data by race and taking a more humanizing approach, Sue was able to drive the development of programs that would provide the level of care needed to guide students of color toward meaningful programs and careers.

Sue's efforts are to be admired, for sure. Having known her and seen her in action for years, I know her impact runs deep and broad, but it didn't happen overnight and certainly didn't come without a price. Over the years, she had to endure politics and resistance when she made it a point to be at the table for every key decision, and certainly, she is a rare IR leader even within the group of incredibly thoughtful IR colleagues I've come to know and interview. The complexities and politics entailed in the IR work are intensifying now more than ever. While the larger DEI movement earlier in the pandemic appears to have brought critical use of data to trend, long-established politics and norms mean that there are still major hurdles to overcome. This is often subtly implied or overtly expressed by my IR participants. When describing how the larger DEI efforts helped accelerate interest in using data, Jill's excitement was underlined by a hint of skepticism: "I think a large portion of that has been through the diversity, equity, and inclusion efforts that, for the first time, faculty are interested in knowing student success data and student access data about different students of different races and ethnicities, and they used to not care at all."

## CONTENDING DATA INTRICACIES, POLITICS, AND ASSUMPTIONS

Nonetheless, this new, complex reality propels institutional researchers to engage in the difficult, yet rewarding charge of balancing the demands for data, the politics and biases involved, and their own evolving sensemaking of what can and cannot be inferred from the data. The increase in data gathering and distribution has changed how IR professionals and other college staff and leaders look at, think about, and interrogate institutional data. Maureen, vice president of institutional effectiveness, who has served in faculty and other leadership roles at Midtown College, described this transformation: "We're looking for data to tell us more nuanced and specific stories about our student subpopulations, but it always comes back to: What are you gonna do about it once you know that information? Which comes back to our strategies. It's all tied in together."

Yet the higher demand and use of data do not equate to problems solved due to the complexities, assumptions, and types of inferences being made (or not). Back to Jill—she was developing a survey for students to gauge their preferences for different instructional modalities beyond the pandemic. While Jill sees the immense value in what data can do and the stories they can tell, she also understands that students are unique and complex humans in their own right, not to be constrained by one or more data points: "We're trying to quantify this, or at least quantify what students think and we recognize the students might say one thing and then do another." Jill's insights were not only in reference to the challenges of making sound inferences due to the difficulties in reconciling what students think and report on a survey and what they actually do in terms of their behavior and decisions; but equally concerning to her were the assumptions and politics flooding in among faculty when interpreting the data. One group presumed that *all* students would want to resume in-person instruction. Another group of faculty expected that *none* of the students would be inclined to come back for their courses in person. Thus, while Jill embraced the data work, "trying to get some of that information about what helps people perform best," she continued to contend with the messiness, including entrenched politics, behind real solutions that can only be gleaned in part from even the best possible data: "You're just not going to find it in the data, has been my key takeaway. People are going to have preferences for reasons you can't predict at all."

As Jill and others outlined these challenging intricacies and politics inherently embedded in the interpretation of data, when data do exist, there is also much to be learned from how IR and other professionals push back on colleagues and engage them to grapple with bias and assumptions when data are absent. Take Boricua when, in his role as assistant dean and registrar at Afton Community College, there were initiatives emerging around financial supports for students to cover tuition, fees, and other living expenses. This was exciting to Boricua, as he knew how much his students needed that extra help. However, one of his colleagues questioned whether the students might be receiving the grant on top of other tuition assistance, or "double dipping," so to speak. He was quick to point out the "deficit" assumption in the skepticism, especially when no evidence was being brought to the table: "This is where data becomes important because if they would have provided me the data to say, 'Hey, these are how many students that have received this type of fund. And then, additionally, this amount of money from the grant and either they're not succeeding right, they're not completing the course,' then I would say, 'OK, we need to look at this differently.' We don't have that data, and you already came into this conversation with an assumption that someone is double dipping."

This assumption became an educative opportunity that spurred efforts to collect and examine information on the students receiving those types of funds toward a "data-informed decision versus an anecdotal decision on what we essentially may be thinking." Boricua also recalled the rewards of engaging colleagues in such ways and "challenging them to think a little differently." For him, dealing with these hard-to-address issues by naming them, and through thoughtfully producing and using data to reach equity solutions, proudly remains his "legacy of being equity-minded and practicing equity in everything I do," which extends to his current role as vice president and chief student services officer, as I described in chapter 3.

These complex rewards and tensions are exemplified by my participants' narratives of the fast-expanding data requests during the pandemic, including environmental scanning, new services, and gathering feedback from students and staff. These experiences inspire them to collaboratively pose important questions to refine practices for the purpose of serving those who historically have not been well served in the educational and employment systems. Encouraged by the imperfect but authentic and collective efforts at her college, Lauren described how acknowledging and focusing on change can ground the nonetheless politically laden data work: "We were looking at policies and procedures with an equity and inclusion lens. So we needed to make some quick changes to make sure we weren't standing in the way."

## REFLECTIVELY ENGAGING DATA TO
## GUIDE EVERYDAY INNOVATION

Grounded within but far transcending IR is my participants' collective new understanding that reflective and thoughtful engagement with data has to guide impactful change in the routine lives of faculty and those in student support roles. In Sue's words, "Any analysis we do is to help the people who are the practitioners to understand their own practice better." Given capacity constraints, cultivating a data culture for equity to guide everyday practices is very much in order. However, compelling as this mentality is, in the realities of how colleges function, many high-stakes decisions were made based on anecdotes, even among the seemingly data-savvy faculty. Shawn described this irony when sharing his new approaches that put a stop to the long status quo of *not* grounding decisions in data:

> Making data-driven decisions, that's something that you would not think would be a challenge with STEM faculty, but that is reality. There is a lot of decisions that are made anecdotally, on anecdotes. This is what I'm seeing, or this is what I feel. But rarely does someone say, "OK well let's go get the data. Let's look at the data. Let's analyze the data and then, let's make a decision based on what the data shows us." You would think with STEM faculty that'd be like a no-brainer, but in practice that's just not what we think first, just like this is what we see in our classes, and we need to come up with a solution to this.

The problem Shawn observed didn't deter him, as he recognized that smaller ways of collecting data can still be powerful in guiding day-to-day activities. For example, he developed a "getting to know yourself" survey before each of his classes, which gave both him and his students the opportunity to discuss and reflect on seemingly small and yet consequential things that shape a community college experience, like knowing an advisor's name to develop a relationship, making progress in course credit completion and in the areas needed to finish a program, how many hours a student works each week, and if the student has caretaking responsibilities for family members or significant others. He then responded individually to each one, citing data to show that these students and those like them actually can and do succeed, especially those demonstrating tendencies and mindsets characteristic of first-generation or other underserved students: "'Do you want to tell me anything else?' You know you get the students like 'I don't know how to do college,' or 'I'm really nervous. I'm forty years old. I'm going back to school, and I feel like everyone's like younger than me.' And it gives me opportunity to say, 'Actually, most students... you're actually in that demographic that has actually historically performed well. So, you'll be fine and here's why. You have all these lifelong experiences that you had. You had kids and you had to learn to adapt.'"

Shawn's example touches on several key approaches to engaging and using everyday data for equity: collecting data on one's own practices and students' experiences, disaggregating data, equity-minded sensemaking, developing interventions, and importantly, getting down to the myths and assumptions that students may know of or have and setting them straight with sound data that motivate students to succeed. Embracing and diving deep into the data in these incremental but impactful ways form the beginning of broader shifts and transformations that get at the heart of long-standing challenges.

While Shawn's efforts are commendable, facilitating changes in data use should not be a process undertaken by a solo individual act; instead, it requires strong academic leadership that is willing to hold all faculty accountable. Carl, dean of science, technology, engineering, and mathematics (STEM) at Inland Community College in the West, described the guided conversation he used when talking about persistent inequities in student progress. He challenged faculty to break down their course data and not only look at how students of color were doing, but what faculty were doing about it: "We continue to see that over and over again that

Latino students and Black students tend to perform, not as well or not as successful, as other students. And so, we want to know, when you disaggregate the data, what is that telling you, then what can you do to ensure that those students are making progress? How did you begin to reduce that gap? And what is your *so-what*?"

To bring the ultimate *so-what* to further light, Maureen emphasized the vital role of contextualizing data to identify root causes of inequities, not settling for just having the numbers: "So I think that's a really important part of it, that being data-informed, we thought we were going to do a touchdown dance and be like, 'Whoa! Everybody wants data all the time. Are we great?' No. Number one, it's too generic; we gotta start disaggregating it. Number two, we got to make sure we know the root causes and once we get there, we got to make sure our strategies match the root causes. So we're getting there. You know it's a cultural shift."

Engaging in such a cultural shift also involves challenging dominant narratives. Mateo, who recently stepped into a service role related to equity and organizational change at Keystone College, saw "inequities—the systems that maintain particular demographics, more disparate frameworks" playing out in faculty's day-to-day practice and the mindsets in which they operate. He described how, over the past several years, there had been a slow but steady cultural shift in faculty mindsets when using data as a space to challenge false assumptions that tend to revolve around who the "typical" college student is and what they want and need, often based on the majority group. For instance, Mateo pushed back on simplistic interpretations of outcomes data, the conclusions made based on that information, and how assumptions can affect critical access and services for students: "What do we assume students want, and what's that assumption based off of? Is that the dominant culture, the majority, and what about people that don't fit that narrative or don't fit that sort of demographic? So, definitely persistence, success rates within courses, and accessibility to whatever that student needs to be able to thrive within their educational program."

Beyond challenging traditional ways of interpreting data, in order to bolster daily practices guided by data, it is also important to accept and honor the diverse forms of data that lend more context and dimension to students' holistic experiences. Earlier, Shawn's example illustrated how the creative use of multiple forms of data (student qualitative input, institutional data, and instructor input) can be empowering for both students and instructors while being integrated seamlessly into the authentic course context. Now, taking a deeper look at Boricua's vision of the use of multiple data types together to achieve a fuller picture and better solutions to challenges, he said: "Let me be clear that both quantitative and qualitative data are important. They should complement each other, and they should not be used against one another. To me, those are the data points that become important to us because it helps us improve." He also cautioned against the use of data to punish faculty and staff. In a sense, any data points that do not signify a positive trend could be misconstrued as negative, with some sort of penalty attached. This is not an uncommon sentiment and fear, as community and technical colleges historically have been situated outside the box when it comes to traditional measures and performance indicators.[5] Even so, Boricua seeks to change this viewpoint: "Many times, data is used as a punitive measure. No, data gives us a realistic perspective of where we are and helps us to identify where we need to go. We need to stop using it from a punitive perspective."

Emerging from the insights and experiences of Shawn, Maureen, Boricua, and Mateo are both incremental and bold approaches to regrounding educators' daily work within reflective and critical use of data. They involve pragmatically tapping sound educational spaces to infuse data as a point of intervention and motivation; they compel educators to challenge themselves and colleagues to resist the tendencies of defaulting to dominant, deficit ways of thinking; they highlight the vital role of accepting and producing diverse forms of data; and ultimately, they motivate everyday work to be purposefully linked, through data, to doing better as a college and for the students.

This new vision of engaging data to transform the everyday is epitomized in Liz, a math instructor for fifteen years at Trailhead College, who underwent her own transformation with data use as an educator. Although she strives to learn about her students "as a whole, and as individuals, as actual people," and to provide sound experiences to support them, even Liz "was a resistor" to engaging data within her own equity work in math. Through experiencing her growth journey and embracing her vulnerabilities, she came to see data as something very real, something that transpires in her students and the kinds of supports she wanted to build for them. Liz described how engaging data to realize her commitment to students transformed her: "Something underneath has shifted it in me. Something very different around the way I listen, the way that I'm open to learning these new things." There was no going back for her after that. At her college, there were ongoing issues with student success in math, resulting in initiatives to restructure math sequences. The data coming out of the initiatives were promising; equity gaps were closing. While Liz was ecstatic, she also made sure that her colleagues had the data in hand so they could see what was happening with their own eyes and feel empowered to make changes. As we have seen in this chapter, data can be critical to helping faculty hone in on meaningful and effective adjustments to their curricula and practices. So Liz took the data, disaggregated and all, and put them in front of her colleagues. It was a "really hard space" for them to all be in, with emotions and tensions, blame and responsibility, but the data served to facilitate collective learning, reflection, accountability, and actions, including her own.

These confrontations with data, albeit difficult, are necessary to achieve equitable innovations and solutions. Although Liz found those conversations with her fellow faculty hard, to say the least, she also emphasized the importance of not being discouraged by what we might find in data. Data are not destiny. Instead, as she said, they present "a way to build your own agency." Liz's learnings from her data journey elucidate how to navigate the challenges and promises that come with reflectively engaging data in daily work. It takes being vulnerable, asking the hard questions, and embracing the productive discomfort of being guided and empowered by data to center students in all ways. As Liz shared:

> I look at my colleagues, and I'm like, "How come you're getting those outcomes and I'm not?" And they did the same to me. So, I would just say, the more that I'm in that space and the more that I'm in a space where that data can be used in a way that gives agency and helps just make decisions. It's not as scary anymore, but it still can really hurt, while there can be discomfort in the data, it is necessary so we can truly engage data in thoughtful, critical, and equity-guided ways. We do this for the students—who are not numbers, but humans who give meaning to the data and the work that we do.

## QUESTIONS FOR REFLECTION

- How can institutions humanize and incorporate more diverse forms of data as an integral part of a culture of evidence?
- How can faculty and staff use instructional spaces, assignments, and other interactive venues with students as real-time data to drive timely solutions?
- What power dynamics and inequities shape data gathering and usage, and how do they affect institutional decision-making and solutions?
- How can education leaders elevate the role of institutional researchers and empower them to center equity as part of a robust culture of evidence within the institution?
- What structures and policies are needed to address politics and power issues particularly related to limited data use and institutional action?

■ How can faculty and staff become active participants and partners in producing and utilizing data for educational innovation and improvement, rather than for evaluative or punitive purposes?

■ What policy measures can be integrated into accountability systems at colleges, where faculty and staff are recognized for their efforts in engaging with data?

■ What policies and practices bolster a robust culture of evidence toward sustained and equitable data use?

*5*

# Reimagine Institutional Partnerships for Equity

*Whether pandemic-related or not, there were many policy windows that kind of opened for us at the same time, and there was a stronger feeling of solidarity with institutional partners where there hadn't always been a feeling of solidarity.*

—ROSALIA, ASSISTANT DIRECTOR OF GENERAL EDUCATION AND TRANSFER, MIDWESTERN STATE ASSOCIATION OF COLLEGES

INSTITUTIONAL PARTNERSHIP is not something new to Rosalia. With extensive experience working in multiple higher education systems and institutions over the past two decades, she has been regularly involved in partnership work, including in her role as assistant director of general education and transfer at Midwestern State Association of Colleges—the state's coordinating body for technical and community colleges—where she provides oversight of general education and liberal arts transfer programs. Ironically, precisely because of her long and deep involvement in institutional partnerships, Rosalia constantly negotiated a sense of apprehension, knowing far too well that at the systemic level, this work often did not live up to its intended purpose: "I think about this all the

time; that oftentimes the [partnership] initiatives that you want to implement at the state level are not necessarily tackling problems that are
there, that are really what the major issue is."

Rosalia's trepidation revealed an enduring duality that permeates
institutional partnerships involving community and technical colleges.
On one hand, there is no shortage of collaborative initiatives spanning
key areas such as transfer and coenrollment between postsecondary
institutions, dual enrollment with high schools, workforce development
with industry partners, and community-engaged work, to name just a
few. On the other hand, despite the great number of these partnerships,
few operated with an equity lens as its guiding principle instead of an
afterthought—a general, long-standing issue in higher education, which
I described in the introduction to this book. As a result, transfer rates
remain stagnant, accentuated by severe racial gaps; dual enrollment continues to be less accessible to low-income students and students of color;
community tends to be disenfranchised; and the workforce/industry
persistently lacks racial, gender, and other important forms of diversity.[1]
Further muddling this duality are deeply embedded politics, stubborn
systems that resist change, and, especially noteworthy, uninformed yet
obstinate stigmas against community and technical colleges on the part
of universities and the workforce. In a word, the "major issue" that needs
to be tackled is often not tackled, despite the hard work put into partnership efforts by dedicated individuals.

Things have started to shift since COVID-19, though, and this time it
felt different, as Rosalia recalled. She brought up a particular example
related to transfer in her state, where, although there had been some
groundwork on creating transfer agreements, during the pandemic,
institutions "came together with partners that they had not traditionally worked with." These partnerships, even with what used to seem
the most unlikely of programs and institutions, grew out of a crisis that
really shifted the transfer conversation. Rosalia described how the university and two-year college systems got all the stakeholders in one place

to prioritize and work on transfer. Previously unimaginable articulation materialized during 2021 that outlined a core set of courses (up to seventy-two credits within the core) that would be transferable among the systems. Rosalia attributed this unprecedented development to two key concerns shared by all—declining enrollment and a sense of care for students, both heightened by the pandemic:

> Everyone seeing enrollments drop, trying to get your enrollments up is like mutually beneficial. And then, really, another aspect was really the focus on the welfare of students. It just so happened that [transfer partnership] work could have very much stalled if it was not given any type of priority during the pandemic. But once again, I think it was something that's all the groundwork had been laid, and then we just decided like we've got to keep running with that. And really *now is* the time, this is the time to support students in their educational aspirations. Less about fighting for the students, and we really did adopt a mantra as a group as an intersystem transfer cooperative. How we've operated was, these are our students, and it wasn't like your students, these students are all of our students.

## A TIME- AND CRISIS-TESTED COMMITMENT TO PARTNERSHIP AND COMMUNITY

What Rosalia shared is a brief window into a palpable theme of partnership and community, cutting across my participants' myriad accounts of change and innovation. Yet again, the pandemic offers a context that motivated various institutions and policy actors to reimagine partnership work with an equity lens. Earlier in chapter 1, I described the vast range of change and innovation burgeoning in community and technical colleges in a Midwestern state. It is worth noting that the range goes far and deep, well beyond narrowly defined institutional boundaries. To note a few of these changes, the colleges extended numerous initiatives to local communities and industries. Responding to limited availability and access to medical resources at the onset of the pandemic, the colleges partnered with industries and organizations in the community to offer protective gear, testing, and vaccinations. They provided or assisted with free vaccine clinics not only to students and staff, but to the entire surrounding public. Colleges also teamed up with community organizations to provide mental health support, food security, and child care for students and others in the area.[2] As described by Chua, an advisor and coordinator for community engagement at Keystone College, "I've seen our community come together to the best of their ability [with] an understanding of the lens of what's happening in our community. So that was always the forefront."

Such partnership efforts transcend state contexts. A quick scan shows that countless COVID-19 vaccine clinics popped up at community and technical colleges across the country, spanning New York to California. Many of these colleges also loaned or donated protective gear and medical equipment, as in North Carolina and Pennsylvania, among other states.[3] These undertakings are inspiring and yet not surprising. Community and technical colleges are historically known for their strong ties to the community and industry, but this mission was undoubtedly put to the test during arguably the most turbulent times in the recent history of higher education. At least from what I heard and learned from these 126 educators, not only did many of the colleges withstand this test, but they also emerged from the pandemic reflexively with renewed insights that illuminate what equity-driven partnerships could look like.

Remarkably, several areas such as transfer, workforce development, dual enrollment, and adult basic education saw collaborative efforts blossom during the pandemic, often with an explicit focus on equity from the onset. Some of these equity-focused partnerships received extensive media coverage, given their high-status funding and national scope; yet many others operated out of the spotlight, doing incremental and persistent work that needs to be shared, elevated, and celebrated. I view these big or (seemingly) small efforts as reflective acts of change that converge at a tipping point to steer institutional partnership out of its stagnant past and into new possibilities where equity evolves into the key anchor. Throughout this chapter, I describe how equity should center innovative partnership efforts across multiple levels—the institutional, student, and relational—toward sustained efforts at the broader structural level.

I want to caution the readers that what I cover in this chapter may seem to heavily revolve around transfer partnerships, and this is a reflection of the prevalent theme that emerged from my interviews. This also mirrors the growing attention to transfer as a policy priority in recent years. All the same, the negotiation of equity concerns, power issues, relationships, and politics transcends transfer and permeates various other partnership types that came out of my interviews. As a whole, this chapter contends with how to enact equity-driven change and innovation in the context of tight college resources through building community and practicing equitable, reciprocal, and generative partnerships.

## FOUNDATION REVISITED FOR PARTNERSHIPS: NAMING AND ADDRESSING STRUCTURAL INEQUITIES

Much as I would love to start with students and equitable outcomes— often the core purpose of institutional partnerships and the ultimate *so-what*—I chose to save that discussion for later in this chapter. Rather, I begin with the proposition that building equity-centered partnerships starts with a systematic-level inward interrogation, where stigma, imbalanced power dynamics, and uneven resources must be named and addressed. Too often, institutional and system partnerships evolved out of either practical reasons, such as enrollment concerns, a genuinely felt need to broaden student options, or both, without first interrogating the historical baggage that underprivileged institutions carry into the partnerships, knowingly or unknowingly, which eventually causes resentment and lack of engagement. For MJ, chief officer at Midwestern State

Association of Colleges, this all felt too familiar and almost personal, even after the materialization of the recent statewide transfer articulation described earlier: "For years, the two-year colleges [in the state] were not motivated. A lot of our institutions had no interest." MJ and her colleagues were not motivated because of the age-old misperceptions of community and technical colleges as an inferior sector and the power dynamics with four-year institutions—all something she experienced firsthand, having worked in the state legislature and several policy leadership roles in state agencies. In those capacities, MJ witnessed that the universities were seen as "superior" and the "drivers of education and higher education change." They were viewed as the institutions with all the "good ideas and expertise," all of which, according to MJ, can make partnership work difficult, if not altogether demotivating, for community and technical colleges, especially when they are perceived as never quite measuring up to their university counterparts.

## Disrupting Misassumptions and Bias

The types of bias and tensions that MJ described are not unique to her state, or anything new at all for that matter. However, when the pandemic hit, it brought all this hidden baggage to the surface, making it crystal clear that it was high time that these unresolved issues were no longer swept under the rug. We can't deny that historically, there are contentious politics and power issues around articulation and partnerships.[4] On the university end, there is a lack of initiative, understanding, and respect for the quality of community college education and transfer students. So the uncomfortable truth is that, for transfer partnerships to work, more than and before anything else, we must disrupt norms and power structures in such a way that power and authority are distributed equally among community and technical colleges and their university partners.[5] My participants shared impactful examples that illustrate how to achieve that equal and trusting partnership. And this is the perfect opportunity to introduce Mavis—a personified window into how to accomplish this feat through organizational approaches that disrupt misassumptions and transform relations among partners.

As assistant director of admissions and transfer at Heartland Consortium, Mavis facilitates efforts toward building transfer pathways and partnerships among community colleges and universities in another Midwestern state. Before that, she worked as a transfer specialist for nearly two decades across multiple four-year institutions, where she was similarly active in building collaborative transfer initiatives with community colleges on a smaller scale. For Mavis, achieving equity in partnership starts with the disruption of misassumptions and bias. In this case, these are the same old misperceptions about community and technical college education. Mavis helps counter them by sharing evidence that says otherwise—evidence on transfer student success, evidence about community college faculty and their rich professional backgrounds, and evidence as reflected in the rigor of course syllabi or programs. She said, "So it's conversations with faculty. And what arises in that conversation is all the myths our four-year institutions have about community college students, curriculum, and faculty. I get to personally address those myths and provide evidence to them to kind of dispel those, and they start thinking about transfer students in their institution."

Once university faculty were exposed to evidence that challenged and corrected their previously held misperceptions, things changed, as Mavis described. Learning success stories about transfer students, university faculty often were compelled to rethink their assumptions. Through looking at the syllabi, they actually identified many similarities between their courses and those of community college faculty. As Mavis articulated, "So I think our [university] faculty were quite impressed with the credentials of the community college faculty. When they heard the depth of understanding of the field that was put into their coursework, that was enlightening to our faculty." She took a similar approach to presenting programmatic information at the department level to open up conversations and address misperceptions: "Hey, you do know, they have a great psychology program at [community college]. I looked at it, and this is how stuff would transfer in." In addition, she readily provides faculty "reports and data showing that transfer students do succeed." Mavis's examples highlight how partnership can start with broadly engaging evidence that dispels the long-standing misassumptions about community college faculty, their courses, and transfer students that perpetuate inequities in transfer partnership work.

## Recognizing and Honoring Institutional Contexts and Realities

Addressing inequities in transfer partnerships also involves the transfer-receiving institutions recognizing the realities that community and technical colleges face, such as varying organizational structures, programmatic and course regulations, limited resources, underfunding, and competing missions, and ultimately respecting and working with these realities. Unfortunately, this rarely has been the case historically. Maggie, a math instructor at Grassland College in the South, described her frustration with university-centricity in even well-intended transfer partnerships: "They want to be supportive of community colleges, but they don't know how, and they don't get it. They're like, 'We love our community college people and want to be involved with them.' But you're not giving us anything that makes sense for us; even your language doesn't make sense for us. I have your [partnership interest] form; I don't know how to answer these questions because you wrote the questions based on your lens, like even just like ranks of the faculty and things like that."

Maggie's frustration shows that when universities come into a partnership without trying to truly understand and operate where the community and technical college is, it can actually create more barriers and make the relationship challenging. Veronica shared her lessons along these lines. As a professor of math and director of science, technology, engineering, and mathematics (STEM) programs at Gateway University, Veronica has been leading a transfer partnership with local community

colleges for over a decade. During this time, she has increasingly appreciated the challenges and constraints that her community college partners
dealt with on a regular basis, many of which she never encountered in her
own work at the university. A case in point was when she first initiated
the transfer collaborative in STEM fields of study between Gateway and
the community colleges in the local area, and computer science was identified as one of the key pathways since it was a long-existing bachelor's
degree program at the university and seemed like a robust STEM transfer
choice. However, over time, Veronica's eyes were opened to the reality that
some of her community college partners did not offer programs that fit
neatly into strictly defined "computer science" categories and thus "seamlessly" transfer. This reality was largely owing to state and institutional
regulations and accreditation standards that restrict the colleges from
developing such programs, rather than lack of rigor in her partner institutions' education or talent in their students. In fact, the partner institutions' information technology (IT) courses and programs are robust and
align well within the larger STEM education and career pathways. So one
of the partners went to Veronica to explore the possibilities.

Veronica admitted that she initially hesitated, being intimately familiar with the roadblocks at her own university, where IT programs were
not recognized as computer science or part of any currently approved
transfer program. While there was synergy, the two different institutional realities produced a significant hitch in the transfer line. But
sharing her community college partner's fierce advocacy for opportunities for transfer-aspiring computing students, Veronica chose to let her
partner's realities guide the many conversations that ensued and lis-
tened keenly and honestly. She reflected on her takeaways and lessons
learned through this process: "Every system is done differently at each
institution; that there's a different institutional context and how things
get done, how resources are allocated, and so that brings a humility."
This ever-deepened sense of humility helped Veronica "step back and
say, what are the top priorities? How do they fit with what my colleagues

at each of the community colleges are doing and knowing that they're doing this on top of all the other things that they're doing?" This sense of humility also empowered Veronica to center her community college partners, their contexts, and their priorities as she advocated within her university to work with her partners' realities. After many deliberations and much effort over the course of a year, Veronica and her partners established a new priority for the transfer collaborative that focused on aligning student aspirations, course selections, and academic support within the larger computing pathways, part of which involved the active development of a new articulation with Gateway's data science program. In the end, the community college reality became Gateway University's reality, and the IT students now have a real shot at transferring and earning a bachelor's degree in their field.

Veronica and her community college colleagues showed what's possible in tackling the thorny issue of articulating programs and courses in transfer partnerships, particularly in STEM areas of study, where there is a stubborn mismatch between the community college courses considered STEM and those designated as such at the university. Veronica's willingness to humbly listen to her community college partners and to learn about and work with community colleges' realities went a long way toward making her partners feel that they were understood, respected, and a true partner. "They really value what we have to say" was the throughline across all my interviews with her community college partners during my site visits. But beyond the personal level, and even more noteworthy, Veronica's collaborative journey of learning, listening, and changing illuminates how to better navigate curricula, courses, and programs that account for the contexts and realities community and technical colleges contend with on a regular basis. Accordingly, rather than expecting institutions to have the same structure, organization, function, and capacity, Veronica and her team came in with a desire to understand rather than assume, which allowed partners to truly get to know and support one another while forging a more equitable and synergistic relationship.

These challenges and insights about how to disrupt power and inequities extend to other domains of partnership, which I cover next.

## Overcoming Stigma and Infusing Equity into Industry Partnerships

Although power issues have been particularly salient in transfer partnerships, given the historical and hierarchical perceptions within these educational sectors, similar challenges carried into other types of partnership as well, such as in industry. For instance, the issue of the community and technical college stigma can also pervade relationships with local corporations and organizations. Meanwhile, some community and technical colleges might view industry as incongruent with the needs, experiences, and goals of their students. These historical issues saw new and promising solutions, as my participants described shifts in perceptions and approaches that lay the groundwork for more authentic, trusting, and equity-guided partnerships. It is about coming together and innovating in ways that are mutually beneficial to students and industries now and in the future. In the words of Todd, dean of STEM at West Grove College, "Looking at industries and corporations as our partners, not as enemies is something that we need to think about more and is the efficient [way of] moving forward for higher ed."

In actuality, viewing one another and collaborating as equal partners are easier said than done. Ethan, a biology instructor at Oakwood Technical College in the Midwest, gives us a glimpse into this when working on a new program. He and his colleagues reached out to some of their industry contacts for input, as it was important for the team to create a program that would meet the local industry needs. Although one of their contacts was willing to help, they didn't mince any words of skepticism. As Ethan told it, they said, "Well, we've never hired associate's degree people. Can they [your students] really perform with what you're saying?" This reaction led Ethan and his colleagues to get out in the community, along with their students, to introduce them to potential partners and show them who they were and what they were capable of as a way to eliminate the stigma. Starting several years before and continuing all the way through the pandemic, they worked on this effort using various innovative approaches, like offering public seminars that brought in world-renowned scientists who talked about their research. Another was a regular symposium that showcased students' work on antibiotics discoveries to regional community members and industry leaders. Making the institution, its faculty, and students more visible in the area helped show organizations and businesses the rich expertise and knowledge residing in the college. Ethan was bursting with pride: "A lot of our [local] employers are now going, 'Oh my gosh, these kids are amazing!' And they just steal them."

In this case, partnership work looked different, in that it was the community and technical college that both centered industry needs and had to dispel stigmas while trying to build a program and forming relationships. While Ethan's story ends on a positive note, these institutions should not have to perpetually prove others wrong just to get on equal footing when engaging with partners. Going a step further, equity-driven partnerships with industry must also look different in the sense that, as institutions of higher education, community and technical colleges should not only listen to their industry partners, but now more than ever lead the partnership by shining a light on what the industry might need in terms of the core skills and competencies required for a reenvisioned future of the workforce. Back to Renee, vice president of academic affairs and faculty development at Keystone College, who is always thinking ahead when it comes to her college, the programs it offers, and the jobs students will be stepping into: "We always say we're preparing students for jobs that don't yet exist. That was years ago, and it was true then." While change is an inevitable part of the workforce, the pandemic sped this up exponentially, she further elaborated:

> Things are changing so fast in terms of industry innovation, technology, and what students are gonna need to know and to do, whether they're

welders or nurses. Knowing that even industry can't tell you what we should be doing, because they don't know. They can only say what they know. And then we have to somehow translate that into—what does that mean, what does that mean for competencies, what does it mean for curriculum development to get those student competencies, how do we measure that? I do think that these transformative last couple of years have been the greatest gift that higher ed might ever get.

A critical prospect for amplifying these opportunities is the shared interest in infusing equity into partnership work. Virginia illustrated this point by describing the increasing industry interest and buy-in for efforts that center equity. A biotechnology instructor at Keystone College for over two decades, she helped establish a new dual enrollment techni-cal diploma program in biotechnology during the pandemic, using an online format involving virtual instruction along with robust lab kits and equipment that students could use at home (or wherever they needed to use them). It was an initiative intended to reach underserved individuals in the area. An industry partner awarded a grant to support this work that allowed them to purchase equipment and offset transportation costs for those students who couldn't afford to come to campus. What's striking to Virginia through this experience was the increasing focus on equity that she saw in her industry partners, which she described as one of the most positive things that came out of the pandemic: "The ability to draw our industry partners into these initiatives is huge. And I think the hook for them was the equity piece. They like that we're reaching out to under-served individuals in the local area. But they really like the idea that we could maybe go further afield and reach out to rural districts that don't have the same resources. And so, I feel like this really helped get employ-ers interested." In this example, the equity vision championed by Virginia and her college appealed to the industry partners' growing awareness of and commitment to equity, which enhanced and enriched the partner-ship. Virginia further described how the college's investment in various types of technology during the pandemic drastically diversified the ways in which employers interacted with students. In-person and on-campus used to be the only modality, inherently limiting access to such opportunities as it benefits more resourced and privileged students. But since the pandemic, the increasing emphasis on equity, supported by the college's expanding technology infrastructure, changed even the most old-school employers. "Our industry partners were now so willing to help us out with virtual presentations, and those have only gotten better because of the investment on the college's part in different types of technology. So the partnerships have grown because of this too," Virginia said.

### Rethinking and Recentering Community in Partnership Work

As we have seen so far, there's been headway toward a clearer vision and approaches to centering equity in partnerships with other educational sectors and industry. Yet relationships with community members and organizations are more obscure, if not largely overlooked. Although community and technical colleges are historically anchored in their local communities, how partnership with community plays out is complicated. Claudia, in her capacity as coordinator for student services at Midwestern State Association of Colleges, brings this issue front and center, seeing how partnerships unfold (or not) leading up to and during the pandemic. She acknowledged that many of the institutions she works with express a strong commitment to community involvement and integration, but they still have "a long way to go." She did not hesitate to point out less-than-ideal relations, including essentially nonexistent ones with marginalized communities at the system and state levels: "Some colleges have better relationships at the local level. We have very little attention that gets paid to other communities in our state."

As someone deeply rooted in service to communities in her professional and personal life, it was clear to Claudia that partnership with community tended to equate to industry or educational institutions in the area rather than actual community members or groups. In doing so, the unintended consequence was that institutions were essentially driving these members and groups away instead of coming alongside them in an equal partner capacity: "Why don't we have an advisory committee that's not only made up of employers, but that's made up of key community players? To really align what we're doing with their needs? I think we align very well with employers. We do not align very well in their communities." The questions and critiques Claudia raised call attention to tough realities that prompt us to rethink this type of partnership work.

The reckoning with these inequitable, if not altogether nonexistent, relationships between colleges and communities has prompted some changes over the past few years. My participants shared budding efforts that often involve the establishment of committees or working groups that do include community members. While I recognize that forming such task forces in and of itself doesn't guarantee real change, and the road ahead is still far and long to travel, I must also honor my participants' enthusiasm about such developments as unprecedented opportunities to position them to advocate for and grow partnerships between the colleges and those living and working nearby. As an example, Chua described a new community engagement team launched at Keystone College in 2021. As a Hmong woman, she considers community a huge part of her life and passion, which was further underlined by her relationship-centered vision as a longtime advisor at the college: "I love getting input; it is so important that the community lies in my work." Taking on her new role as the team's coordinator was a full-circle moment: "I'm excited to be doing this work because for the first time I felt like—now I can include a community voice, in any way, shape, or form, that to me is engagement, right? Having them help how we shape our policies and institutional practices." In addition to the engagement team, Chua shared how the college is looking to form an advisory board comprised of various community members, including those who identify as Hmong, to better understand and serve those living in the area. It is about bringing everyone to the table, especially those who have been marginalized, and amplifying their voices in the partnership to fully real-ize the "community" part of community college. As Chua put it, "We're all in it together, even though it seems like we're not; we are all trying to really fight and dismantle barriers so that we, so that our institution can do good for the community."

As these educators navigate the promises and challenges of partnership work, they all face the critical question of what it takes to achieve equi-table partnerships across different domains and stakeholder groups. MJ offered a valuable reflection in this regard: "I think what it takes is the con-vergence of stakeholders, the convergence of stakeholder demands, and to truly be successful, just like any other effort, the practitioners have to be participants, willing participants. This is something that I truly believe, as someone who wants to see the four-year higher education sector not just survive but thrive. It is something that I hope they will embrace, part-nership and transfer for lots of reasons, but equity of opportunity most importantly." While MJ was speaking of partnership in relation to trans-fer, what she said rings true across all partnership types. Equity should be at the forefront, with each side paying respect and giving due credit to one another as willing, equal partners, with an equitable distribution of power. The COVID-19 crisis prompted a long-overdue reconceptualiza-tion of partnerships with equity as an intentional centerpiece. This is not only significant for partnerships in and of themselves, but also for tack-ling long-standing inequities among students, which I discuss next.

## THE ULTIMATE *SO-WHAT*: HOLISTICALLY TACKLE STUDENT INEQUITIES

As I alluded to earlier, an equitably and carefully crafted partnership sets the foundation for addressing core equity concerns that students face—the ultimate *so-what*. However, the experiences or pathways created by partnerships often ended up being more convoluted than intended to be. Elizabeth, vice president of learning at Midwest Technical College for nearly four years, hit the nail on the head through her reflection on all the hard work that goes into building transfer partnerships with local universities, only to have students continue to not have their credits really count. In her new approaches to negotiating partnerships, she is calling out the fact that these feel-good agreements are in fact not serving transfers, and the thorny core issue—credit loss—must be addressed: "So, trying to work with our partners to make sure that we don't have students—it's still an ongoing conversation—how do we make sure that our students who are coming into the four-year university aren't losing a whole semester of time and credit hours, which is common even in what we've said are great transfer agreements? I don't know how they call them great. Students are still losing these fourteen credit hours." Similarly, Sharon, vice president of academic affairs at Parkfield Technical College, discussed the importance of revisiting and innovating transfer partnerships to ensure that the agreements actually transfer what they intend to, without students losing out on credits, program progress, or other benefits: "It's got to be innovation in the curriculum, so it's course-to-course, program-to-program, standard or not, or however you do it. How many ways can we articulate inarticulable courses?" For Sharon, nothing was allowed to fall through the cracks anymore in the transfer process. She was determined to close any possible gaps to progress toward a truly seamless transfer partnership for students.

Such concerns motivated my participants to pursue partnerships carefully and unapologetically, centering what's best for students. As Elizabeth's example already indicated, this starts with a critical assessment of whether university partners are serious about creating a transfer process that does not penalize students by setting up additional barriers. Take Anthony, executive director of student services at Parkfield Technical College for the past six years. He shared a new approach in recent transfer partnership efforts that scrutinizes four-year colleges' commitment to ensure "equal value" transfer for students and a truly "direct and seamless transfer" before students even step onto the Parkfield campus: "In what we're doing in trying to attract our partners, not so much attract, but to measure them, and then make a decision on who our partners are, we're being very, very candid that we are really out looking for the best situation for our students, and it's kind of on them to show us how it would look and how it would work."

Surely, a partnership is meant to amplify the support and chances of success for students, not complicate it. Naming this from the onset, before entering the partnership, sets up the foundation for a holistic vision to address the unintended and yet enduring inequities that students experience in partnered pathways. Back to Mavis, who was determined to approach the partnerships she led differently and beyond the "transactional" level. Rather than the usual review, rubber stamp, and on to the next thing, she believed that there needed to be more to the transfer partnership process: "A lot of the transfer pathway work that's happening nationally is pretty transactional in nature. You get your faculty together, they review the coursework, they approve the coursework, you put it in a guide, and you hand the guide out. Done. What I have learned over time is that it has to be more holistic in nature." There needs to be a real, reflective questioning of the substance of those partnerships and whether and how institutions, faculty, and college staff are serving students on all levels, especially once they make it to the four-year college or university. Mavis added:

> So what this does is, it gives me an opportunity to specifically connect with faculty at our four-year institutions, and to raise the issue of how are transfer students doing at your institution? Are you recognizing those students in your major? Are they transferring in well? Are you able to connect them to your institution early? Things like in the STEM majors; can they get into research right away their junior year? If they are going into business, can they start to connect with those first-year internships as a junior so they can do a more advanced one as a senior?

These hard and action-oriented questions exemplify a holistic vision that transcends a one-shot, transactional approach, delving into some of the most persistent inequities of the articulation process and transfer student access and experiences from a global and long-range perspective.[6]

Innovations aimed at addressing inequities in students' educational and career pathways and trajectories are not restricted to transfer partnerships. Here, we turn to TJ, a facilities management instructor for thirteen years at Midtown College. He shared about a new industry partnership that would alleviate the consequences of jobbing out—students taking a job and leaving college before they finish a credential—especially among racially minoritized, low-income students who often face challenges accessing and persisting in college due to location and financial constraints that compel them to choose work over education. As TJ put it: "A lot of people in these areas, they're just trying to survive. We have to have a way that they could continue to live as they gain this education." The new partnership would tackle those inequities by bringing the college and industry to the students where they live, to "bring the information about potential careers that many people probably are not aware of." They then encourage and support students to sign up for the building technician programs, along with wraparound supports like child care and transportation, to alleviate their costs and time to attend along with improving their access to jobs and education. Midtown College and industry partners come together to host workshops in those communities and talk about control and maintenance technician work and employment opportunities. TJ added, "Then if people who come into these workshops are interested in these and they want to set up for classes at Midtown, we're going to connect them with these funds to pay for their schooling. At the same time, they start their classes, I have six companies lined up to hire them part-time with the potential to get more lined up to do this." Having forged those industry partnerships in ways that put equity at the forefront, many of the stubborn economic and racial inequities in students' education and careers are being tackled.

With the majority of the program cohort being students of color, TJ has proudly brought some of them back to the college as instructors: "I look around the room when I'm in our events, and I can see equity."

A similar long-standing equity concern is found in dual enrollment partnerships regarding access based on location, especially among low-income students and students of color. David was proud of Central State College's new math outreach program, which not only extends access to dual enrollment offerings, but also ensures that students are substantively prepared for college-level math. David shared that the college hires math faculty to teach in the high schools and the courses are fully aligned with those foundational ones offered at the college: "So, students are more likely to be successful in their first college math course. We're preparing more students for the first college math course, and that's huge."

David's sense of pride is well founded, as the issues addressed by the program sit at the intersecting core of several key equity concerns around dual enrollment: inequities in access and math preparation, which all too often are racialized, as students of color enroll in college at lower rates and tend to be tracked to less rigorous math preparation prior to college.[7] The racial equity gaps manifested through dual enrollment and other areas are also a top concern for the college, David shared. The program is leading the way in not only making college preparation and courses more accessible to students who otherwise might not have had the opportunity, but also setting them up on a positive educational trajectory at the postsecondary level. Additional dual enrollment partnerships are growing in other areas toward greater access to college faculty and courses, especially core courses in general education such as English, psychology, history, and sociology.

Central State College's dual enrollment innovations reflect a larger ongoing effort among my participants' colleges toward alleviating inequities through high school–college partnerships. In the words of Ruth, the president of Crosswind College, a community and technical college in a rural area of the Midwest, "I'm like, let's figure out a contract so we can do dual credit. I don't take no for an answer; we will figure it out. I'm looking forward to that work and being able to provide those things for our area." Prioritizing equitable access to dual enrollment and other opportunities among her rural students, she has been actively working to create more flexible educational options through high school partnerships. Like Ruth, many more of my participants are keenly aware of the significance of partnering with local public schools, striving to do what it takes to ensure greater, more equitable access to college pathways.

Equity concerns also motivated new partnerships engaging with the community. David elaborated on another new effort to provide equitable access to Central State College for its widely geographically dispersed students through public transportation: "So, you think about, in response to transportation challenges to physical proximity, something as simple as an ID badge, which you can now show and ride the bus for free." The partnership did not stop there. The badge was the first step, followed by working with the local transportation services to develop additional routes "deeper into the community to increase access to our campuses." David admitted that some may view this effort as "simple," and yet simple is also innovative, as it is that simple solution to what appears to be a simple problem that ultimately enhances access—"that ultimately increases the number of students because the college campuses are pretty widespread. So I think that's a great, innovative partnership with the community in terms of the bus system." Tackling disparities and gaps in students' access and experiences, these examples shared by my participants demonstrate that when partners put equity first in their relationships and innovations, everyone wins, especially the students.

## CULTIVATING RELATIONAL SPACES OF PARTNERSHIP

To realize the equity goals at both the structural and student levels in a partnership, it takes relentless effort by the people in it, who constantly interact, negotiate, and recalibrate with one another across various contexts. What's more, these relationships must transpire in carefully cultivated relational spaces to process biases and grow some of the most innovative and powerful possibilities. When I asked Mavis about what has driven her ever-evolving vision over her decades of transfer partnership work, she responded: "So holistically, I think of it in terms of not only who touches the student along the way, so advisors, faculty, the admissions person; but where that student is learning and growing and discovering who they are. Those people also have to be part of this conversation." Mavis brought up the make-or-break of a partnership—the people in relation not only to students, but also to one another.

So far, I have talked about the foundation and the *so-what* of equity-centered partnership. Connecting to both and underlying everything in between, though, is that rich, deep, authentic relational space shared by the people in the partnership.

Earlier in this chapter, I described how, through sharing evidence, Mavis was able to help address misperceptions of community and technical college faculty and students. What was not lost on me was how she achieved that not only through looking at data and evidence, but also by bringing people together. While respect plays a huge part in negotiating these relationships, Mavis promotes dialogue in shared events so that faculty can get to know one another, their work, and their courses. This helps remove misassumptions and foster authentic partnerships because at the end of the day, "it's just like any other assumption you make about somebody until you have a personal interaction and experience to dispel that myth, that myth exists," she reflected. While there is no doubt that Mavis has moved the partnership forward by leaps and bounds, she does not view her work as a solo act: "You can move things along as an individual, but you have to develop, find, discover the other transfer champions on your campus and connect them into the conversation. I believe that small steps can have huge benefits in moving an institution along, but you have to consistently have some champions in place taking those small steps."

## Creating Stable Institutional Structures to Facilitate and Sustain Relational Spaces

Getting to know the people in a partnership is crucial, but it's just the beginning. To sustain partnerships, relational spaces must be carefully cultivated, starting with creating stable institutional structures that would allow the connections made to become more stable than relying solely on the so-called organic interactions. For Mavis, this means having specific individuals from different areas of the college, such as enrollment, academic affairs, and faculty members who are regularly connected to one another and the students: "So, I actually have three key people for every major: a staff person in enrollment—someone who's in the front line talking to transfer students every day, the faculty contact for that particular major, and the academic affairs contact that kind of give their blessing in this work and the authority to do this work." There are additional touch points that occur throughout the process, like marketing or the registrar—all made smoother through the established relationships with enrollment, academic affairs, and faculty.

But most essential of all is creating stable structures that keep faculty involved and connected. Mavis pointed out: "If you really want to start to address the needs of transfer students and to move your institution from transfer friendly to transfer receptive, you have to have faculty involved. We're moving to more of a professional way of, how can our faculty at these different institutions start to connect?" To facilitate faculty involvement through stable structures, Mavis has actually found herself playing matchmaker with faculty from community colleges and four-year institutions to "learn about each other's programs, learn about their personal experiences, passions, knowledge as a professional in their major area." She shared some of the ways that faculty connected, including virtually through platforms like Zoom, which was especially useful during the pandemic. Once they were able to meet in person, regular professional development sessions and visits also were put in place to facilitate relationships among faculty. Mavis explained: "So like all the psychology faculty will be meeting for a professional development meeting, sharing their work across institutions. Also, we are starting our lab visits, so we have four-year institution faculty going to visit community college faculty in the labs and see what their labs are like and learn about their programs."

## Navigating Relational Spaces with Respect and Humility: Asking Questions First

In navigating these relational spaces, it is especially important for more privileged institutional partners to be reflective and open. Veronica commented on how she learned and adjusted her approaches as a university leader on a transfer partnership working with her community college partner leaders: "Asking questions first. That was really to try to save their time to allow and respect their individual structures of how they wanted the work to transpire. Another point of meeting with the community college colleagues is those human connections that help you work together to reach our goals, and if they know that you really want to know what they need and listen to them, that helps the work." This relational aspect applies to other partnership types as well. Samantha, a chemistry faculty member at Midwest Technical College, described a similar approach to connecting with local industry partners on a relational level by putting their needs first: "We've been able to interact with our industry partners so much more. We ask them every advisory committee meeting, 'What do you need? What are other gaps that we can fill?' Sometimes the gaps that they want us to try to fill, we can't. We just don't have the equipment. That's OK. They get that. We try to make sure we're giving them what they need from our students and preparing them that way." Asking questions, really listening, but also acknowledging and respecting the realities that various partners face, go a long way toward sustaining strong and authentic relational spaces.

## Cultivating Relational Spaces and Partnership with Community: Listening and Learning

Entering into relational spaces with an open mind and respect also extends to partnerships with community. Claudia, at Midwestern State Association of Colleges, offers us some history and context of community relations in the state, particularly regarding adult basic education. Although one of the core functions of community and technical colleges is adult basic education, the individuals they serve are often isolated from those institutions "to the point that there are people who still will say those are not our students. They're not college students." This mindset can be extremely damaging, as it indicates a lack of relationship and creates barriers for these students in accessing degree programs. Claudia noticed that many of the institutions in the system tended to focus on all other kinds of partnerships when it came to students and enrollment, with adult basic education students left out of the conversation. And this is despite the fact that there are "[adult education] students right here who desperately want to come into a program, and they can't, they haven't. The colleges don't have solid pathways for them to be able to do that, or it rests on the shoulders of their GED instructor to make sure that they can get through." As a result, she saw a huge need to better understand and improve the bonds with the communities that come in contact with the colleges through adult basic education: "When we talk about equity and inclusion in our institutions, we need to talk about adult ed populations as included."

Claudia's concern was deeply shared by Clive, an organizational effectiveness specialist at the same association. For both, cultivating relational spaces to learn and listen in is key to reimagining relationships with communities. Clive described the monitoring that the association does with the adult basic education programs, such as English language learning, to report to the state's education department. He views this capacity as extending beyond a monitory one and reenvisioned it as a relationship where everyone comes alongside one another toward continuous improvement. In this new vision, there is a "kindness," as Clive put it, instead of a hard-and-fast compliance, to help the programs align with expectations and requirements. During the pandemic, feeling the craving for kindness and community, Clive further cultivated relationship spaces in new ways by coordinating drop-in listening sessions every other week, where community members and organizations could "let down their guard, talk about challenges, talk about obstacles, sticking points, successes, ask questions of the group." These sessions continue to this day. Using the listening sessions as relational opportunities helped Clive "create a space where folks could just talk, invent, and brainstorm, and just let things kind of naturally, holistically emerge rather than me shaping that agenda." In doing so, he demonstrates the value and impact of embracing community toward building relational spaces that cultivate true partnerships.

Throughout the process of navigating these relational facets in institutional partnerships, it would be naive to assume that tensions and politics don't show up; they do. Just as Mavis said, "They have different mindsets, different needs, different fears, different triggers." Similarly, Clive acknowledged these realities and his efforts to support conversations—and partnerships—going in fruitful directions: "There's been tensions with politics in some of the work that we do but it's easily avoidable, depending on how you message the information, and your intent, and the support you provide alongside it." At the end of the day, the anchor that steadies and deepens equity-guided partnerships is to position everything in discussion within the perspective of how students navigate and are affected by partnerships. "Otherwise, they do nobody any good, especially the student," as Mavis put it. Her comment rings true across the educators in different partnerships, as they all seem to be contending with this one big question: Does the implementation of promising partnerships purposefully ensure access for all those whom they are intended to serve, especially those who have been repeatedly denied educational opportunity historically?

As she recapped what she and her colleagues accomplished, Rosalia reminisced about their shared sense of solidarity: "Whether pandemic-related or not, there were many policy windows that kind of opened for us at the same time, and there was a stronger feeling of solidarity with institutional partners where there hadn't always been a feeling of solidarity." This solidarity is a grounding thread underlying the partnerships described in this chapter that was rarely felt before the pandemic. More important, as the participants shared, this sense of solidarity serves as a catalyst to initiate more open dialogue and troubleshooting with the goal of dissolving some of the most stubborn barriers in partnerships. The seemingly unprecedented progress in removing these barriers also opens "many policy windows" toward a common goal within the larger higher education ecosystem, which allows various stakeholders to reimagine and renegotiate their roles to prioritize complementarity over competition through building and working in productive and respectful relational spaces. Meanwhile, these educators grapple with how to be more intentional and student-centered, as well as what it means to infuse equity into innovative partnerships and avoid unintended consequences that only perpetuate inequities. All told, my participants, through their evolving efforts and breakthroughs, show us a reimagined institutional partnership for equity as an act of support, collaboration, and reciprocity.

## QUESTIONS FOR REFLECTION

- What can be learned from the experiences of the educators covered in this chapter to inform policies and strategies that prioritize student-centeredness in partnership work?
- When engaging in partnership work, what institutional, industry, or community contexts should be considered to foster equitable collaboration?
- What misassumptions and biases exist in partnerships, and how can these insights inform future strategies for partnership development?

- How can individuals utilize relational spaces to develop stronger interpersonal connections toward robust and equitable partnerships at scale?
- What policy measures can be implemented to address inequities in partnerships? What policies and supports are needed to bridge infrastructure and resource limitations faced by partners?
- How can innovative, equity-guided partnerships extend impactful practices into institutions, industry, and communities?
- What partnership practices and models effectively and equitably support transfer, completion, job placement, and other measures of success defined by institutions and/or students themselves?

# Build a New Institutional Culture with the Kindness of Humanity

*That's something we can't be scared of; to say our people need to be loved right now.*

—Alberto, president, West Bank College

THROUGHOUT THIS BOOK, I hope I've made clear the commitment to serving students embraced by my participants across varying roles in direct and indirect student support. In many cases, times of crisis further bolstered this dedication with a sense of solidarity, as you have seen from chapter 5. Also running deep though is the undercurrent of burnout. In chapter 1, I described the alarming duality of fired up and burned out that touched nearly all faculty, staff, and leaders, who were often enthusiastic about efforts to better serve students, only to eventually realize that they were running out of steam. As faculty looked back on what they had to push through, their long sighs, fatigued looks, and stirring narratives gave away the deep burnout that they were experiencing. In the words of Brayton, faculty director at the Center for Excellence in Teaching and Learning at Keystone College: "I think there's been real faculty fatigue, like in a big way." Kayla, a nursing faculty member who also serves as a coach at the Center for Teaching and Learning at Midtown College, further unpacked how during the pandemic, faculty life caused a range of burnout sentiments felt and exhibited among her colleagues:

> So I'm burned out right now. I have experienced burnout. I don't know if everyone has experienced it, but we are all facing challenges, and we must be mindful and respectful of that for everyone. And to just have more compassion and understanding for people. Some people did require more understanding than others. I think that's important, to understand that this is temporary. And it's impacting everyone, whether they realize it or not. Some of them don't recognize it and can't acknowledge it. Others recognize it, and don't acknowledge it because they believe it would make them appear weak.

This mounting phenomenon extended far beyond faculty and resonated deeply with all my participants. Staff members, especially those in student services capacities, negotiated equally draining times with amplified student needs, extended availability, and evolving modes of support. Boricua at Afton Community College in the South reflected on this growing issue among his staff and colleagues working across various student support roles:

> What I've come to assess is I think burnout has become elevated for many of us because of the modality of how we're supporting students. What I mean by that is there was the time, before the pandemic, where students weren't reaching out or meeting with us virtually. Everything was in person in our offices, and during certain times of the year, you had your peaks and your valleys as it relates to activity in certain offices. I think that's where some of our student affairs personnel now are experiencing burnout because now there's a new way of connecting and communicating.

Boricua's insights put into context how the pandemic had thrown off the ebb and flow that would allow educators to handle intensive moments with the prospect of restoration.

The new realities have become even more unsustainable for those particularly in tune with the growing equity concerns that affect minoritized students. Claudia at Midwest State Association of Colleges pointed out that, while the awareness and recognition of equity issues have greatly increased, it came with a heavy tax on the group of colleagues she closely worked with—those who held positions in or were specifically involved with efforts around diversity, equity, and inclusion (DEI): "The amount of work, like physical and emotional work that that group is being asked to do, has not changed and has increased. With the combining of the COVID-19 pandemic with racial violence that continues, people in those positions are just constantly on. Helping students, supporting students, the ones who are going to lead something and respond to something and the college, and so that's the group I think I've personally seen the most burnout and adjustment."

## A PANDEMIC WAKE-UP CALL: FROM FIRED UP TO BURNED OUT TO THE GREAT RESIGNATION

The parallel theme underscored by personal commitment and collective burnout is both logical and paradoxical. It is logical given the obvious toll the pandemic has had on educators. In the earlier chapters, I already detailed how they stretched further than they could to offer greater flexibility and holistic care to their students. This deep student-centeredness that runs up against a penetrating weariness is also paradoxical. While compassion, flexibility, and urgency to do things differently are take-home lessons for everyone at the individual level, in most of my participants' colleges, the lessons have not collectively transpired in a new institutional support culture to alleviate faculty and staff burnout. Overall, a thread that is conspicuously absent from both participants' own accounts and analysis of voluminous media sources and institutional documents is systematic, sustained support and development for faculty and staff.

This reflects a widely shared, looming concern. As argued by educational researcher Kevin McClure and colleagues, many in higher education navigated daily challenges that led to burnout, discontent, and even resignation.[1] While some of the specific challenges were spurred by the pandemic, collectively, these issues are a reflection of longer-standing, deeper, and pervading problems around work expectations and norms, treating individuals as expendable, inequitable compensation, and demoralization. In the community college context, these issues are further underscored by the heavy emotional labor that institutional members, especially faculty, are expected to perform, as argued by Leslie Gonzales and David Ayers.[2] The constant work and worry have only been brought to the surface by the pandemic, the severity of which was named and recognized by nearly all my participants, including institutional leaders themselves. Overseeing the Center for Excellence in Teaching and Learning at Keystone College, Lauren has perhaps the most holistic perspective on faculty burnout:

> I think the faculty were going through a lot. We're still dealing with burnout, and how much do we put on the faculty, even now. We're so appreciative of the great lengths they went to over the last two years, and still today, to make sure the students are taken care of, and I mean they're the ones that did it. This is an intense experience. They attended Blackboard trainings, usual trainings, like they really tried to equip themselves best to be able to continue to teach students in the remote environment. They were exhausted, and they did everything they could.

Recognizing the magnitude of collective burnout, Lauren was also deeply worried: "Some concerns I have are how the faculty are feeling? Now, where are they at? What can we do to continue to support them? Because they are the critical individuals to make sure that students get what they need in the classroom, and they graduate, and they pass their exams and move on into their careers. I worry about the faculty. I worry about resources. I worry about the innovation that we started during the pandemic that we need to be able to continue."

Because of the unrelenting expectations, shifting guidelines and policies, overwhelming workloads, and no space for respite, many chose to leave the institution. Maureen's observation as vice president of institutional effectiveness at Midtown College elucidates the intricate interplay between staff departures and burnout: "The turnover has been hard, and then burnout. We seem to always ask the same great people to do the work. The people I ask to do retention grants, they were also the people who were already working on funding distribution, and that was massive." Maureen brings to light how turnover ends up amplifying burnout since it is often the same individuals who are being asked time and again to step up and take on more and more. Lindsey, a chemistry instructor and program director at Walt County College in the West, took note of the compounding convergence of burnout and departures that inequitably affected those who tended to carry the biggest share of the load: "For those of us who've been here as long as we have, the amount of people bailing in the past few years is off the charts. And you know what's messed up? The ones who've been here forever and were our go-to peeps, they're gone too. It's like losing your backbone, the ones you could always count on." Couple this with what Claudia mentioned earlier, the relentless faculty and staff efforts to address equity in their work and support students bring them ever closer to burnout, essentially nullifying the essence of what they're doing as it is not sustainable in the long term.

## TOWARD EQUITY-DRIVEN LEADERSHIP
## CENTERING CARE AND VALUE

The Great Resignation that is happening on many campuses, accentuated by and contributing to unaddressed burnout, serves as a huge wake-up call, as faculty and staff can't continue to fill others' cups when their own are constantly empty. Obviously, as shown in the examples of Lauren and Maureen, institutional leaders feel the pressure to create the structures and supports that both energize and retain staff and faculty, but I don't want to reduce an issue of such magnitude to a simplistic take on leadership. Now back to Renee at Keystone College for a moment. Her account embodies the emotions and commitment of herself and her counterparts, who are leading, teaching, and serving through all the turbulence and undercurrents described earlier. An approach that seems so genuine and yet is so rare, Renee made it part of her practice to contact at least ten faculty members a day simply to check on them via email. Her message was simple and pressure-free: "Just thinking about you, how are you? That's it." The faculty would often reply with what Renee described as "profound insights, struggles, and inspirations," which then essentially served as an authentic and creative venue for her to gain critical, timely feedback from faculty.

Through this messaging of care, Renee informalized and thus transformed her long-standing human-centered approach, continuing to deliver on her promise to ensure that her faculty members feel seen and heard. But Renee's innovation and humanity as an executive leader came with a human price too. She experienced severe exhaustion over the past few years and ultimately decided to retire early. Renee's example reflects the perennial leadership challenges facing community colleges. Marilyn Amey and Pamela Eddy highlight the difficulties of leadership in responding to changing environmental and organizational contexts, all the while staying true to the multiple missions and stakeholders they serve.[3] These changes and challenges require leaders who are dynamic, adaptive, anticipatory, and innovative. However, the existing nature and norms of leadership, if left unchanged, can result in an unsustainable workload and climate, as what happened with Renee. These issues brew into a perfect storm that eventually leads to weariness, leaving the leadership role, and maybe even departing the college altogether.

The alarm bells regarding community college leadership retirement and turnover began several years ago and are only growing louder. Renee was only one of the many tangible examples. Reflecting on his own experience and the shrinking time span leaders are spending in their positions, Alberto shared, "I think something that we'll be seeing over the next few years is the amount of tenure that our presidents have at an institution. Especially anybody who started during the pandemic, for that group of leaders, looking at how long they lasted the institution that they moved to, because I have a feeling that's gonna be short." These leadership challenges not only come at a human price but also underscore a critical human value that was being brushed aside, leading to the burnout and resignation at all levels that have since crept in. Brayton compels all institutional stakeholders to have important conversations with one another when determining the structures and rewards that are most meaningful: "What does it mean to feel valued? What does it mean to feel safe or protected and appreciated? And I think those are conversations that will need to take place, as we grapple with coming out of the pandemic."

My participants' descriptions of their experiences and sensemaking of the pandemic burnout serve as a crystalized window into some of the most enduring challenges facing institutional culture and structure at community and technical colleges that will require equity-guided, innovative institutional leadership that cares for and values everyone, including leaders themselves. Especially notable among these challenges are the elusive and evolving nature of faculty work, as well as trust issues among administration, faculty, and staff. In the following discussion, I engage these challenges as key contexts for developing innovative, adaptive leadership practices that support, engage, and inspire faculty and staff. I also outline practices and suggestions toward embracing the future of work and professional development in community and technical colleges—which are underscored by flexibility, trust, empowerment, and rejuvenation.

## The Elusive and Evolving Nature of Faculty Work, Underlined by the Issue of Trust

An institutional culture that truly cares for and supports its people comes from a deep understanding of and empathy for the nature and demands of their work, a general lack of which is the root cause of why most of my participants don't feel they are seen and supported by their institutions and continue to suffer burnout. There are several areas of faculty work in community and technical colleges that serve as prime examples of just how the work is elusive and constantly evolving, ranging from shifting workloads, roles, and instructional approaches to critical professional development to keep up with student, industry, and community needs and demands. Although many of these areas represent enduring challenges, the pandemic complicated faculty work in a multitude of ways and created an even more unsustainable environment for it.

Norms, expectations, and demands for versatile modality of teaching have changed forever. On the one hand, these changes appear to open up possibilities, as pointed out in chapter 2. On the other hand, online learning is not as easy as it looks or sounds. John, vice president of academic affairs at Pointe College, described the tricky delicacy of this new reality: "Online learning is incredibly flexible for the learner. It's also incredibly flexible for the instructor. It's a hell of a lot more work than a face-to-face class, in my humble opinion." Virginia, a Keystone College biotechnology instructor, also pointed out the complexities of navigating burgeoning learning flexibilities and her own reservations: "In many ways, it feels like we got all these pieces together and we're ready to go. And yet it could just be a total bust because we don't understand how students are feeling. And that's, I think that's actually the largest problem." Faculty were especially inundated with new learning technologies during the pandemic, trying to get a grip on how to use them and deciding which would be in the best interest of their students.

This is one of the main reasons underlying faculty burnout, confusion, and frustration. Most institutions' current version of supporting faculty is to dump on them all kinds of resources, and on occasion, more extended professional development related to using them. Linda, a biology instructor at Keystone College, described the information overload: "The college just, they sent us a lot of links, 'Here are some ideas,' and some of us felt like, wow, actual tools would have been nice." Although there is value in supplying plentiful resources and ideas, many faculty members do not have the time or incentive, on top of their already full workload, to engage in trial and error to determine which resources are applicable and helpful to their individual situations.

In cases of more thoroughly established professional development, faculty, even the most inclined, are "just burned out on professional development," according to Michelle, who uttered this sentiment in light of all the investment in professional development at Coppice College, providing in-person and online support and peer mentorship, along with stipends. A peer mentor herself, Michelle observed a flagrant lack of participation among her colleagues: "Nobody comes. Nobody. Faculty aren't coming. They're too busy to come to professional development now." Being busy is certainly not a new issue for faculty, which further muddles the prospect of building valuable professional development within their existing roles, responsibilities, and schedules, as voiced by Marie, a biology instructor at Keystone College: "To be quite honest, I don't have the time. [Professional development is] great, but for all of those things, there's always that question: How do we operationalize that within what we already do?"

It was at the juxtaposition of all this burnout, evolving yet elusive responsibilities, and lack of systematic institutional support that trust emerges as a tested attribute that further complicates the uncertainties and changes faculty face in their work. In many ways, the unexpected quarantine, waves of swift decision-making, and intensive labor visible to faculty and staff but not always noticeable to others presented challenges in trust among faculty, staff, and leaders. Ethan, a biology instructor at Oakwood Technical College, described how faculty work was approached at the beginning of the pandemic at the college level, and how that changed over time: "Things were super flexible at the beginning, but as the pandemic dragged on, that flexibility started dwindling and came this whole issue of trust, you know? That the faculty were teaching from home; are they really giving it their all from home, or should we make them come back to the office? The administrators just couldn't shake that sense of mistrust toward the faculty."

Similarly, Ashley, a psychology instructor at Skyview Technical College, shared her frustration with her institution's distrust of faculty during the pandemic: "We do not need to be present forty hours a week. Trust me to do my job. You trusted me to hire me, then trust me I can do my job when I'm not physically in front of your face." Crisis situations have justifiably caused strain and heightened tensions across all areas of our life, higher education included. However, it is all the more crucial to ramp down those pressures and concerns through a message that says, "You all are doing a great job. I'm just gonna keep my hands off. I trust you to do your job," as Ethan put it. In doing so, institutions can retain critical trust and avoid further exacerbating burnout and discontent.

## Rethinking Support and Development for the Future

My participants laid out valuable takeaways about how to put structures in place that honor the shifting nature of faculty and staff work, and how to reinfuse and further shore up trust rather than letting it erode. First, in order for community and technical colleges to encourage their people to rise to the evolving and changing terrain that is even new to them, there is a need to rethink what support and development really mean. When critiquing his institution for missing the mark in terms of supporting faculty, Peder, a graphic design faculty member at Glacier Technical College, offered a compelling shift in perspective: "I would just ask if they [college administration] consider faculty as being their most important assets. Please keep in mind that your faculty are your biggest resource." This perspective, positioning faculty as assets, beseeches institutions to treat them as such—to be treasured and cared for. In the vision of Helen, vice president of Midwestern State Association of Colleges, this means taking a break and the space to sustain and amplify the brilliance of staff and faculty: "Their plates are full. Quite frankly, during the height of the pandemic, they were 24/7. They were accessible. They were very productive, ultra, high performers. And I'm like, OK, you folks can't keep going at that rate without tiring. So you need to stop out, you need to do self-care so that you can continue to be brilliant. Otherwise, your brilliance will burn out, and I don't want that."

This intentional pause or pulling back enacted by leadership demonstrates care and commitment to protect faculty and staff as the assets they truly are. Similarly, at Keystone College, Renee strives to model for all her deans and others the mentality of taking something off the faculty plate. For her, developing faculty members to be impactful and innovative teachers doesn't start with adding more, especially now, but rather with pausing, stepping back, and resting. Reflecting on Renee's leadership which centers care and value, Lauren captured its gist: "I think our vice president [Renee], she really was constantly the advocate by relaying that message—where are the faculty at right now? What can we *not* ask them to do?"

Taking things off their plates does not necessarily mean inertia in faculty and staff development. Rather, given the fast-evolving nature of these educators' work, professional development support would need to ramp up, just in different ways. A tangible approach toward addressing this tricky trade-off—not adding more but continuing with professional development—is to repurpose some of the existing but stale professional development venues and the current structures of performance review at many colleges. For example, in-service days are a prominent format of existing professional development that require one or more mandatory days set aside for faculty to participate in a set of activities. Yet my participants found limited value in them when the in-service days were mostly set aside for presentations and meetings that centered around institutional goals and priorities—lofty speeches often detached from what challenges and supports the day-to-day work. Instead, these in-service days that faculty are required to attend could be revised into community or collaborative learning venues where educators can focus on a particularly timely and thorny topic or issue and work together toward actionable approaches and solutions.

Disgruntled by how unmotivating the current in-service days are, Ethan provides a sketch of what this might look like: "As faculty members, we face the students and know our students best. If we collaborate like that—just having the freedom and the flexibility to meet, we will be able to start at the bottom and have some small collaborations, some small things. And see if it works, and we will know right away whether or not it works." This type of collaborative learning in community with one another has proved to be an especially promising strategy for faculty development.[4] Thus, repurposing existing professional development venues into more meaningful models, as Ethan explained, can yield great value and joy of learning in community, without adding yet another item to the faculty's and staff's very full lists of to-dos.

A synergistic idea is to rethink what counts as work time, especially for faculty. In the current model, professional development in the community college often takes place outside of faculty work time.[5] The same applies to other added roles and responsibilities, which are tacked on to their existing workloads. While some institutions find ways to compensate faculty for some of these activities, time and capacity spent in response to the many emerging developmental needs are hardly accounted for. Ginger, an agriculture instructor and department head at Nova Technical College, spoke of the new landscape of faculty development involving curriculum development and online learning: "If there is a focus going forward of doing online, making sure that the hours that are put towards that as teaching hours truly is reflective of what you do in that capacity. Because, as we know, it just takes longer to do that."

Ultimately, holistic faculty and staff review may need revisiting to be more of the moment and closely tethered to the essential aspects of the work. Several states have review systems of teaching, academic, and occupational requirements or competencies that faculty must meet in order to teach at community and technical colleges. As an innovative example illustrated next, the faculty evaluation mechanism could serve as an optimal platform that integrates faculty review with professional development and support, as at Midtown College, where this review system is housed within its Center for Teaching and Learning. The support piece comes in the form of coaching and peer mentoring, which have helped make the process feel less like a requirement and more like a developmental process, as detailed by Casey, director of the Center: "And so having our coaches do that work with their peers is amazing. So their peers are helping them develop teaching and learning materials they're giving them feedback on. They're not like judging the quality of what they've done. That's what they're doing with their peers, which to me is a great way of going about things, and I think it helps all the faculty learn. I think that the programming and the support that we're able to offer is fantastic because it's coming from peers. They know what each other needs." This approach serves the dual purposes of meeting state requirements and providing timely, useful professional development, while not adding more burden and instead efficiently creating richer opportunities.

Further, professional development in this dawning era doesn't always require new, shiny tools. In fact, open, reflective, and collaborative spaces for dialogue and learning or unlearning can be most empowering and rejuvenating. Maureen talked about a new practice at Midtown, where leadership across key functional areas gets everyone in the same room, with a focus on listening and learning from one another and using those lessons to help them develop and grow. One example that she highlighted was the president at her college regularly gathering together multiple units and staff for honest and productive conversations around what went well and what did not while adjusting to the pandemic, all with the goal of improving their work for the benefit of one another and their students: "Our leader [college president] put us in a good position to have safe space for innovation. There was such free dialogue and we learned so much that we could serve people, staff, faculty, administration, everyone better."

## Letting Trust Transpire in Faculty and Staff Work

A reimagined model of support for evolving faculty and staff work is also one that is characterized by trust. Trust as an action instead of rhetoric. My participants described tangible approaches and directions for trust to transpire through impactful communication and infusing flexibilities in meaningful ways, ultimately reinvigorating development and support for everyone.

Trust starts with clearer and transparent communication for faculty and staff to better understand and align with priorities and expectations, explained Virginia: "As colleges move forward after COVID, how do the plans that the colleges have actually get transmitted to their faculty and staff, because sometimes it can feel like, 'Oh, the college has no idea,' but really, they just haven't communicated what their plans are going forward. And so, you sit there and have this initiative that I'm working on, but if the college's priorities are shifting in this way because of COVID, then maybe I should just stop that and move in another direction?" Several leaders expressed parallel lessons learned that came out of the pandemic, such as Rose R., interim chief academic officer at Nova Technical College: "I just think that transparency is absolutely key. I think it's building trust. I think it's building strong relationships with the staff that I have. So that's a really important piece so that's kind of the leading down but leading looking up." Or take Maureen at Midtown College, who highlighted changes in communication prompted by COVID-19 that paved the way toward greater transparency and trust: "I believe our processes for communication have become much more agile, recognizing the importance of anything that's going out to all employees. I'm ready to answer your questions. I'm not doing that 'I don't know, somebody made a decision' kind of thing. So I think our communication processes really stepped up and they had to."

Trust also means giving faculty and staff the flexibility that they need and have proved to thrive with. My participants shared that flexibility—as reflected by putting structures in place that honor the shifting nature of their work, like remote work and scheduling options—was a significant gesture that demonstrated trust in faculty and staff, which allowed them to flourish and avoid burnout. At Midtown College, for instance, the institution decided to enact more work flexibilities with faculty and staff. Although this was an initiative that grew out of the necessities of the pandemic, it also demonstrated trust by allowing individuals to continue the option, as described by Sue, director of institutional research: "Because a lot of people were able to show they were able to work from home effectively, the college actually formally put into place a policy procedure, the flexible work arrangement. So people can discuss with their supervisor, like I will discuss with my employees about what's the best schedule for them. So then it's kind of trying to show the employees the trust from the college, but also because there's a lot of research that shows the productivity, like reduced commute and then more productivity."

While these kinds of flexibility were important to survive COVID-19, maintaining them in the long run can lead to a deeper level of trust and flourishing. Alex, dean of transportation at Nova Technical College, also pointed out that such flexibility signifies a trust in faculty and staff to do the work that needs to be done, which goes a long way: "Having that relationship built with my teams and being able to really trust those teams to do the work, that they're the experts. And I think that's what it comes down to. It really comes down to trusting the people that are going to do those things."

David, provost at Central State College, discussed being intentional and thoughtful moving forward, including showing "flexibility in the work schedules that really responds to the complexity of their [faculty and staff] lives, while optimizing learning and our resources and the capacity we have." Athena, associate vice president of academic services at Lakefront College, described a similar approach to extending flexibilities beyond the pandemic to alleviate the burnout that had been brewing: "Could we look at that [remote work schedule] and then try to schedule the major meetings where we really need you in person on those days of the week? I think this is what's worked best with a lot of the folks."

In addition to flexibility with regard to remote work and weekly schedules, Nova Technical College went a step further. Wade, president of the college, found that such flexibilities were so well received that his institution is looking into additional avenues: "I think flexibility throughout the entire calendar year is something that we're continuing to hear. On our support staff or administrative staff side, the ability to work remotely when and how they can but still meet the needs of our students is important. So we're going to end up being a pretty hybrid environment for the foreseeable future." He viewed this change as especially important because "if we don't offer those kinds of things, then there's a certain group of our faculty and staff who are going to say well I'll go where we can, or where I can do those things."

## TOWARD INSTITUTIONAL CULTURE AND INNOVATION BUILT ON THE KINDNESS OF HUMANITY

The experiences and lessons I have shared so far call for systemic change and innovation toward structures, policies, and ultimately an institutional culture grounded in humanity and built on the premises of trust and love. A core component of such a culture is affirming humanity and rendering care. Alberto demonstrates this through his conversations and interactions with faculty and staff at West Bank College, being aware of and embracing the very real and complex feelings that everyone experienced and continues to work through as a result of the pandemic: "While we need to adjust so that we make sure that the institution is here long after us to serve students in the community, understand that there's definitely grief, there's pain, there's anger and, yeah, it sucks. That's exactly the language I've used, which is, it sucks. Let's be honest, let's talk about it; not in some sort of academic way, but just in a very real way." It is this sense of vulnerability that has the power to bring people together and strengthen trust and relationships. Alberto strove to be cognizant of pain points and to keep the humanity at the forefront when cultivating and preserving trust: "Not any one of us started this, but we are here to try and resolve it together. It's just keeping the humanity of people in check, and what I've told my leadership team is that this hurts and it should hurt, because the moment that it stops hurting you've lost some of your humanity." So how do we render humanity and care, in ways both big and small, that will be more supportive of faculty and staff, address burnout, and establish the trust and kindness needed moving forward?

## Seeing the People, Nurturing Their Success

Rendering humanity and care starts with truly seeing the people—faculty and staff—as key engines of the institution. Brad, a manufacturing instructor at Prairie College, spoke metaphorically when illustrating this point: "The well-oiled machine sometimes needs the oil changed." Time and again throughout my interviews, successful leaders evolved to be those who see their people, recognizing their burnout and growing pains and working with them to alleviate them. In the words of Marques, dean of manufacturing, agriculture, and construction at Nova Technical College, "Part of this response to the crisis, and having it be a catalyst for healthy change comes back to being flexible with our people. You know I talked about how resilient they were. I also had to really listen and watch people because we were constantly asking them to step up to the starting line again. And we have to make sure they rest."

Giving people the rest and recharge that they need may start with small practices that honor the need to "Zen" as part of their work routines, as reflected in Boricua's deliberate practice of scheduling shorter virtual meetings with intentionally longer breaks rather than solely focusing on the convenience and efficiency of virtual meetings: "I'm sure my colleague needs time to decompress, especially if it's a meeting that's a little bit intense if we're talking about a student situation. I think in order to address some of what we're seeing, we have to identify different practices in ways that we can be better supportive of our employees that are feeling the burnout." Behind Boricua's small example is the larger direction toward disrupting the dominant, often unquestioned business model devoid of care for staff, and starting to transform it into one that prioritizes care.

On a more developmental and human level, Brad further captured the value of checking in on faculty and staff for any challenges that arise, and when they do, using those challenges as growth opportunities toward a nurturing, kind, and trusting culture: "Being a leader, keep an eye on your faculty and staff in general, just making sure that they don't have any kind of issues, and if they do then try to grow and learn and assess it and figure out what you could do for it, to be able to make it better and prevent it from happening again." This approach requires not only constant observation, but also reflection and regular adjustments through actively seeking feedback loops or venues for honest conversation. Toni, a faculty member and program director of industrial safety at Keystone College, also highlighted important leadership practices such as listening, empathy, and follow-up when issues come up, as they can affect the trust and culture of her college, or indeed any other institution:

> And when you talk about systemic issues, talking about our experiences and what we went through, and where the challenges were at, you're being pretty vulnerable. I understand if people don't really know how to empathize necessarily with what others are saying, but there's still some way to build in a little bit of empathetic talk, or things like that into a facilitated discussion like that. And if people bring up

a concern, or you tell them about something that's going on that's not going to be addressed until a later time, you need to find a way to close that loop with them.

Truly seeing the people also requires attentiveness and being in tune with what motivates them and makes them successful. Precious, dean of health sciences at Afton Community College, centers her practices around just that—not only with those on her team whom she interacts with on a daily basis, but also with each individual she encounters across the institution: "You have to truly spend time with understanding who our people are. I need to know what makes them want to show up every day." For Precious and other leaders, this approach allows them to provide the actual means and conditions for thriving. Similarly, Peder likened it to the ways that the college should approach student success: "So give these people all the tools they need to be successful, just like we do to our students. I don't view that relationship as any different from being us and our students and administration and faculty. Give them everything they need to be successful. Be patient and nurture them [faculty and staff] and get them to be successful with their students. Sure, grace in times of crisis, like we went through. And in return, hopefully, that that gets transferred down, that we have that same thing with our students."

As illustrated in this chapter, although colleges have made tremendous strides in instructional adaptions and more holistic student supports, systematically implemented, meaningfully engaging faculty and staff development and supports remain rare. This presents an intriguing conundrum where many individual faculty, staff, and institutional leaders alike continue to commit to the mission of a community and technical college education, and yet overall institutional morale is in somewhat troubled waters. Precious, Peder, and others show us that a student-centered institution should render that same attentiveness and care for the less seen people—the very faculty and staff of the institution—and when their needs are attended to, the impact is felt across all levels.

Toward that end, this chapter describes some notable exceptions; some of them may appear small and incremental, but they all illustrate innovative, adaptive leadership practices that support, engage, and inspire faculty and staff. Such shining cases illuminate how to cultivate a culture of kindness, trust, and equity—a culture grounded in humanity that not only lessens burnout but, more important, honors faculty and staff as key assets to thrive as they continue to carry the bulk of responsibility in service to students.

As we take stock of the challenges of burnout and long-standing educator work issues exacerbated by the pandemic, (re)building an institutional culture with the kindness of humanity could not be any timelier. Alberto reflected on the flexibility and support that must be extended to everyone, but ended on the note of love and empathy: "That's something that we all need to be cognizant of for employees, for faculty, for staff, for administrators; we need to just be flexible and kind, and give people some compassion, some love. That's something we can't be scared of; to say our people need to be loved right now."

## QUESTIONS FOR REFLECTION

- How can educators adopt innovative practices within the existing portfolio of their work to avoid further burnout?
- How can educators balance their roles and responsibilities with their own well-being and professional development needs?
- What changes to work expectations and structures are needed to address burnout exposed and exacerbated by the pandemic?
- What structural changes are needed to repurpose professional development in ways that support faculty and staff as their roles and responsibilities evolve and change?
- What are the key elements of effective professional development in community and technical colleges?

- What steps can institutions take to prioritize the needs and well-being of faculty and staff, recognizing them as key assets essential for student success?
- How can flexibility, compassion, and love be integrated into institutional policies and practices to ensure that faculty and staff receive the necessary care, support, and resources to thrive in their roles?

# 7

# When Innovation and Equity Converge

## *A Case Study*

*Once we start to embrace the student as a person. That's where we're
going to see the best change in our society.*

—STEVEN, FACULTY MEMBER AND PROGRAM DIRECTOR, MIDWEST TECHNICAL COLLEGE

TOP OF THE NOON HOUR on a gorgeous, quintessential late summer day
in the Midwest, and I was about to enter the student success center building, where I was observing the Organic Chemistry lab. There was a hint of
crispness in the sunshine that could almost be smelled, accentuated by
the vibrant display of full-blooming hydrangeas adorning the Midwest
Technical College (MTC) campus. In that moment, my heart was filled
with a profound sense of hope and possibilities that lay ahead with the
new semester, academic year, and future of the community and technical college.

I was midway through my visit with MTC's Science Pathway Program
(SPP). It was among the most humbling and yet uplifting visits I ever
had at a community and technical college, where I witnessed not only
what's possible, but also how to make the impossible possible. It brings

together the best of what a community and technical college can and should offer: transfer and employment opportunities that don't compete or limit, robust partnerships with the industry and universities, an education and support structure that is always at the ready for students, and the perpetual reflexivity and willingness to change and adapt to advance equitable student access and outcomes.

A few months back, after seventy-some interviews with my participants, I sat down with Steven, a biology instructor and program director at MTC for over ten years and someone who came highly recommended as an innovator through my network of community and technical college colleagues. Steven is one of those faculty members who had experienced it all: worked in the biotechnology industry, had a full-time research gig on viruses and viral engineering at the National Institutes of Health, and eventually earned a PhD in biology. Despite his strong ties to the industry and professional world, Steven's vision of technical education programs reaches far beyond workforce development in a transactional nature, a mission he found to be too limiting going forward: "Yeah, we are preparing people for the workforce. But you also need to prepare them for all aspects of their life. There's so much more to education than just transaction. I'm hoping that that becomes a more popular thought right now."

Steven's vision of equity is one where all his students "learn the science and be able to see it in their everyday lives." He described this as "the ultimate empowerment—knowing that you have knowledge and being able to apply it in your life." Driven by that vision, Steven worked for years to bring human immunodeficiency virus research programs to his campus—a rare innovation for community and technical college students to access. For it to come to fruition, Steven navigated the college's standard administrative processes, which inherently take a long time, while contending with initial pushback. Leadership and fellow faculty had doubts about how research would fit into the college's mission and instructors' roles. But he continued to press his college about the research program until he got everyone on board. In hindsight, Steven realized that stubborn, persistent pushing planted the seeds for SPP: "That's where I'm starting to see some cultural change."

Which ultimately led to the creation of the SPP—a collaboration initially starting with Steven and Peter, an associate dean of general education and longtime biology instructor, and eventually across science faculty and industry and university partners. It is a program that really has it all: a rigorous lab science curriculum leading to noncompeting educational pathways where students can receive an associate degree and go into the workforce if they want, or they can use it to transfer to any of three public in-state universities where the curriculum is fully articulated; inclusive and humanizing approaches to teaching science, grounded in high-impact teaching practices; a built-in internship and a capstone in which students design, conduct, and present their own research, all by the time they finish at MTC. Bolstering all these are holistic supports ranging from meeting students' basic needs (e.g., laptop rentals, financial assistance for child care, bus passes, and gas cards) to proactive advising and faculty mentoring.

And no, this is not external grant-funded work. SPP was started from the ground up by Steven and other faculty colleagues I cover in this chapter. It is funded through the college's general budget, which is how all programs are typically supported at MTC. The funding of other program elements that support students, like laptop rental or gas cards, ranges from departmental or college budgets to, on occasion, SPP team members' personal funds. Over the years, the program navigated a long but fruitful journey in achieving buy-in from leaders and partners in the college, universities, and industry. Reflecting on the SPP journey, Steven went back to the core of his *why* as an educator: "Once we start to embrace the student as a person. That's where we're going to see the best change in our society."

I was sold the second I heard the SPP story. The moment that the school was back in session and in full swing later in the summer of 2022, I hit the road to visit the team at MTC. I attended a number of class sessions, labs, and team meetings to get a glimpse of SPP's various program components, courses, and practices. In between, I interviewed the core group of faculty and staff in addition to Steven: Rose, the lead physics faculty member; chemistry instructors Samantha and Mary; Eve, a biology instructor; administrative leadership including Peter and Gretchen, both associate deans of general education; and last but not least, Kevin, the program's academic advisor, who provides support to both students and faculty. I also studied numerous documents including course syllabi and materials, program description and catalog, advisory meeting documents, and program events information. In this chapter, I share the SPP story with inspiration and humility. It encapsulates some of my best learnings that have evolved out of the larger research. It embodies educational innovation at its best.

## THE FIRST-DAY FUN

*I have to get students in the door, and then, once they're in the door, I have to assess what they need. You have to figure out what it is they need, and then get it to them, so that there are no barriers to learning physics.*

—Rose

My first visit was with Rose in the early morning on Monday. She was teaching Physics II, a class that is part of the SPP sequence and covers the second part of the basic principles of physics using problem-solving, labs, and applications. Rose actually has chemistry and earth and space science backgrounds, but through a series of serendipitous events, she ended up with a degree in physics education. She spent a decade in the K–12 sector and another decade in higher education, teaching physics across various student groups. There was a laid-back aura surrounding Rose, her approach to the class, and her initial interactions with the students. She greeted them casually, gently reminding them of the "no water bottle" policy and making sure that they had "the big white binder," which turns out to be a comprehensive portfolio Rose developed. It contains all the essential course instructions, activities, and handouts, provided to the students free of charge. If any student didn't have one, Rose directed them to visit the bookstore on the same floor to obtain it promptly. Curious, I inquired if these details were already communicated via email before the semester began. Rose chuckled lightly and replied, "Oh yeah, but this is all part of the first-day fun." She went on to explain that she arrived at the first class aware that many students may not have read the emails or instructions, missed out on acquiring the big white binder, or perhaps faced difficulties finding parking and were thus running late. "This is all part of my first-day fun; it's all part of understanding the students' contexts," she elaborated. Humming in the background was the soothing melody of "You Gotta Be," an R&B and soul song by British singer Des'ree.

The big white binder proved immediately useful. After providing a brief contextual overview, Rose swiftly organized the students into teams, initiating an activity dubbed the "Treasure Hunt," with detailed instructions outlined on pages 6–8 of the binder. Essentially, through this activity and assignment, Rose invited students to get familiar with the course and go out with their team members to locate the academic services available to support their physics journey. As someone with nearly two decades of teaching experience, I couldn't help but be astounded by how Rose deftly connected students with all that they bring to a class—life contexts, commitments and responsibilities, prior math experience, program areas, potential challenges, and accomplishments—and all that they need, like knowing course policies and logistics, scheduling, office hours, campus resources, and academic support, just to name a few. It not only tapped into students' unique backgrounds and abilities but also catered to their specific needs. "It is all about figuring out flexible and reliable support for students' different needs and have students taking an active role in their own success," Rose explained later.

Intrigued, I myself embarked on the Treasure Hunt activities, which require students to look for class and campus resources, assuming the role of a first-time visitor and imagining myself as one of the students. All the resources relevant to the class were located together on the second floor of the student center. As I wandered through, I encountered a group of volunteers from financial aid and student services, looking ever-ready to offer their assistance. As someone who often finds myself getting lost and forever hesitant to ask for help, their initiative put me at ease. One of these individuals, Sabrina, graciously accompanied me down the hallway, ensuring that I reached my intended destination. She mentioned that their support initiative had been in place for a few years, particularly since the school gradually transitioned back to in-person classes, when it became evident that students and visitors often struggled to navigate the building.

Back in the classroom, I could feel the energy radiating from each team as they eagerly handed in their completed Treasure Hunt sheets to Rose. But the adventure didn't end there. Rose took her time reviewing every sheet with every student, discussing various elements such as shared acquaintances, daily life and work commitments, family responsibilities, and logistical aspects of the class. Above all, she dove into her students' unique scheduling needs and contexts, especially as it became evident that tutoring played a vital role in the class support system—a real and tangible resource that Rose emphasized repeatedly. As they gathered around a whiteboard, Rose and her students collaborated, marking down the most suitable days for individual students to seek tutoring.

Throughout the class, I was captivated by that same sense of invitation, exploration, and joy of scientific learning. For Rose and her fellow educators, the value of creating a safe and relaxed environment where curiosity can freely flow cannot be overstated. She reiterated this sentiment multiple times, referring to her class as a place where students are encouraged to "blurt it out" and ask questions without hesitation. Such an ethos permeated every aspect of her teaching, from seemingly mundane tasks like explaining the syllabus to demonstrating the use of Blackboard (a learning management system) resources. The underlying focus always remained on how these elements fit into the larger context of students' lives. The whole time, the classroom buzzed with a sense of camaraderie and purpose.

Later in the day, Rose opened up to me about how the pandemic had heightened her awareness of the equity implications inherent in their science program, particularly when it came to the lab component. During the initial uncertainties at the onset of the pandemic, the team's primary concern revolved around the accessibility of the lab and its equipment for students. For Rose, the lab represented a powerful lever for mitigating the inequities stemming from disparate student backgrounds: "There's something about the physical space of doing science in the lab that removes barriers and levels the playing field for students who may not have had access before."

This realization reinforced Rose's conviction that providing access to science education is of paramount importance. It propelled her to further embrace inclusive approaches to teaching, exemplified by her first-day fun mentality and the Treasure Hunt activities. For Rose, teaching physics extends far beyond physics the subject matter—it is about creating an environment that is accessible, less intimidating, and equipped with readily available support to help students navigate the intricacies of the scientific world. This newfound perspective reinvigorated her practice, making her cherish and savor every moment spent teaching. As I returned to campus the next day, bright and early in the morning at 8:30, Rose was back in action, teaching in the same lab. The students were clearly carrying on with their first-day fun, plausibly into the far future.

Rose showed me what an accessible, yet empowering context setting looks like for compassion-enhanced and rigorous science teaching. I later learned that Rose was someone whom the rest of the team looked up to as an expert teacher (ironically, the only one without a PhD). As both Steven and Peter shared later when describing all that they had to navigate in building transfer partnerships, these PhDs "mattered more than they should." Indeed, it's Rose, without those three letters, who inspired the rest of the team about how to teach, support, and care about their students differently. As I continued my visit and classroom observations,

I saw the same threads of accessibility, compassion, and active learning across all sessions, although underlined by instructors' unique backgrounds and personal styles.

On to Mary's Organic Chemistry lab. It was a vibrant hub of curiosity and exploration. As the pioneer of the course, Mary had the opportunity to intentionally develop it from a nonscientist perspective and in such a way that centered access and active learning. Recognizing that many of the students at her college cannot afford to have technology at home or simply don't have it for other reasons, Mary strikes a balance of using technology when it makes sense for students and moved away from requiring textbooks, instead making any texts optional and using her own resources that students could use for the course: "So the students that are in a situation where they can't afford that or whatever don't necessarily need that." She also pushed up against the "standard way of teaching organic chemistry." Rather than the traditional abundance of memorization, she designed each class session to be a workshop where students work in groups to solve problems together, sometimes like games or puzzles, but with plenty of rigor: "I intentionally make the problems pretty challenging, based on what we've done in lecture, and they have to struggle through it and work through it quite a bit. So I try to do a lot of that in my classrooms, in a low-tech way." Having that blank slate allowed Mary to create an innovative organic chemistry course that stands out from the others and supports students' realities, learning, and success.

After reviewing key learnings from the previous class session, Mary had students work in teams for the entire class, drawing out structures of organic molecules electronically on a laptop and using software—all freely provided to the students in the lab. She roamed around, intentionally pausing in the background when teams seemed stuck or there was a particularly challenging problem. She walked students through the steps if they struggled for too long, all the while offering positive reinforcement. Sounds of exhilaration sprung up, and as the students started to wrap up building the structures, they exchanged questions and processes, and on occasion briefly shared experiences about other courses and summer jobs. As everyone finished, the teams swapped structures and compared notes, and this was when Mary pointed out some mistakes by posing guided questions and walking through the steps. There was a general vibe of ease and chill underscoring Mary's attentiveness, and it was contagious, as the students immersed themselves in their hands-on and collaborative projects with focus, confidence, and poise. *Seemingly weightless yet still effortful* is probably the best way to capture the power of the engaging and supportive environment that Mary created.

This sense of support and empowerment carries into other classes, such as in Steven's blended microbiology class. For his first lab session, after settling his students in and going through strict lab protocols, Steven went on to share his academic and professional journey pursuing biology, including saying how much of an imposter he felt like along the way. His story initially took some students aback; the look on their faces showing that they clearly did not expect their instructor to start on such a vulnerable, personal level. However, as he continued unpacking the feelings and emotions involved in research and the countless uncertainties, failures, and joys in the process of conducting science, students became enthralled and relaxed simultaneously. At that point, I sensed that all this sharing was never really about Steven. It was about relatable experiences and emotions.

Later, Steven explained how, after the first few times he ran the course and witnessing student intimidation and fears, he decided to approach it the way he does now: "It's a very emotional course, which, as I look back on it, I should have remembered from my own time; how emotional graduate school got. How you'd feel when presenting for the first time in front of faculty members and scientists. Since then, I always start by discussing feelings. It may surprise some people. Scientists talking about feelings? What are you doing? But it's crucial for success." As the class went on, I saw how starting from a place of vulnerability emboldened the whole class to tackle complex scientific concepts and engage in lively discussions with openness and confidence.

## THE DUCK SYSTEM

*...there are groups of students out there who are underrepresented in the world of postsecondary ed in the STEM world. We can create a nonthreatening and safe way for them to get into science, and then the science will take over and capture them, and they'll be great when they go somewhere else.*

—PETER

In the shared office of Mary and Samantha, fellow chemistry teachers, a unique sight caught my attention during my interview with Mary: piles of small, yellow rubber ducks perched on the bookshelves against the wall. Each duck had something written on it. My curiosity was satisfied the following day, as I sat down with Samantha for her interview. She explained that the ducks were actually inspired by a presentation by their vice president of learning at MTC, who used them as a visual to demonstrate shared responsibility in supporting individual student persistence and success through the college. The SPP team latched on to this idea and asked to use the ducks. Each duck had its own name and represented one of the students in the program. "The duck system made it easy for us to visually see each student, their needs, progress, who they need to connect them with, who needs an internship, who is about to graduate," Samantha explained. Each faculty member has their pile of "ducks," but they often compare notes, she said: "Who has what duck? We just look at the pile. We know when there are issues that come up. We know, OK, this student has these needs. So, we know what to look for." When their students finish the program, they move to the graduate pile. This quirky duck system is no secret, though; Samantha told me, "The students know this exists, and they geek out about it. They think it's hilarious. They love the fact that they have their own little duck." Everyone seems to get a kick out of the duck system, a seemingly peculiar invention brought about by deep care and commitment to seeing students through.

The duck system offers a window into another centerpiece of SPP—its holistic support structure. The first element is faculty mentoring. Mentoring is typically not a formal part of a community college instructor's role, and although it made its way through MTC in 2015 as an expectation for all instructors, it served as more of an encouragement for organic conversations and interactions with students. SPP faculty found ways to further integrate this role at multiple levels. The first of these is that meaningful, personal connection. For instance, Mary described how, being a first-generation college student herself, she was drawn to SPP for the possibility of mentoring students like her: "I'm a first-generation college student and I can relate to not really knowing much about the whole system of academia. I thought it would be a great fit for me to support some of those students that might not have seen a bachelor's in their future, might not have seen a science career in their future, and be able to mentor as part of that."

Having that personal connection as the foundation for impactful mentoring, the team has also grappled with challenges, with one of the biggest being how to reconcile student learning needs and their external contexts that sometimes pose obstacles. Mary explained, "Teaching the content is the easy part. If that's all we had to worry about, our jobs would be so much easier. I think honestly, the biggest hurdle is all of those external things that our students are facing and helping them navigate. That really becomes part of our role as well. Students have all those other things going on that they often bring into the classroom." So Mary started to not only allow but also welcome those contexts into the classroom, just as her student teams were at ease discussing other coursework and summer jobs after they finished the lab task. For Mary and others, science teaching is not to be confined to content; rather, it should integrate other areas of students' lives. When the instructors extend their roles as mentors, there is enhanced access and relationship building for the students, given the established connection through a class context. Faculty mentors described how these experiences helped them and students learn about each other as fellow humans, their lives, and their college journeys. And that provides a strong foundation for holistic learning, holistic teaching, and holistic support.

In offering holistic support, the SPP team does not just view students as passive recipients of assistance; rather, they view their teaching, mentoring, and advising as venues for cultivating relationship and empowerment. We saw this in action through the courses I observed. Now I turn to Kevin, SPP's academic advisor, in an academic advising context. He views himself as "a thought partner for students." By that, he means that he encourages students to develop relationships with those they interact with, from instructors and advisors to other college constituents: "The whole point is that we don't just want to make decisions for students. We want to help them feel empowered in the decisions that they do make. So, modeling that behavior, but also being supportive." Even when engaging the parts of his advising role that he described as "very transactional," such as signing up for classes or explaining credit policy, Kevin is still about empowerment and the big picture: "Even then, we're still trying to get a sense for: Do you understand what it is that's in front of you, as far as the task of registration? Do you understand that ultimately the goal is, these credits can be applied here or there? So always checking for understanding [of the big picture] is an important part of the task."

As a relatively new member to SPP, Kevin admitted that this is the only program that he has worked with that has such a high level of engagement from faculty, which results in a convergence of advising roles that are collaborative and beneficial to students. As an example, Kevin described how Rose often bounces ideas off of him about certain students' advising needs: "Hey, this student had this conversation with me. Here's a need we've identified. Well, here's an opportunity to have a conversation, or what are your thoughts around this?" He also spoke to the impact on the students when instructors use instructional time to point students clearly and confidently to him as the academic advisor in the program: "And the whole idea is, when an instructor can say to a student: 'I know you definitely need to talk to this person, or you definitely need to see your advisor,' that allows students to feel that they're in that safe space. They know what they're doing. So I think we're also trying to create that sense of belongingness by forcing ourselves to have these conversations." And that sense of belonging is what Kevin strives to cultivate. He takes time to walk students through tricky situations and crafts every word in his email correspondence so that students receive his messages feeling love—love for doing education and love in the sense of human connections: "When students come to MTC, they're not buying their courses. They're not buying their education. They want a sense of what it means to be human. It is like 'I want to enter into this space and engage with you.'"

Throughout my visit, I saw the same themes of compassion, love, and empowerment shining through each of these educators' practices and approaches. These elements are indeed part of the larger fabric of SPP, driven by its equity vision from the beginning, as explained by Peter, someone who worked closely with Steven to establish the SPP:

> A very substantial portion of our students have at least one mental health issue, high level of LGBTQ, disproportionately high number of students of color compared to our student population. That tells us exactly what we felt when we built this program, which is there are groups of students out there who are underrepresented in the world of postsecondary ed in the STEM world. We can create a nonthreatening and safe way for them to get into science, and then the science will take over and capture them, and they'll be great when they go somewhere else.

And it was quite a journey toward creating that nonthreatening, safe space that SPP is today. Peter elaborated: "You have to create the pathway, but you also have to be super intentional about the community and that's really hard to do at a big institution." First, there is some unlearning to do, but the best part of that is doing it with a team. Peter described how some of the members of the team, including himself, had to unlearn their past ways of teaching science. He admitted, "I didn't understand when we started, how important [creating a safe space] was going to be. I was kind of with Steven like, 'Oh, they're gonna love the cool research projects.' Well, they do love the science part, but a big part of why they stay is that we create a warm, welcoming, nurturing, nonthreatening environment that allows them a couple of years to build confidence while they're figuring out college and figuring out how to be successful in rigorous classes." Peter credited Rose for helping them eventually arrive at a revised version of science teaching that works for SPP students: "It was the vision Rose had for creating a sense of community and a sense of a quirky belonging identity as part of the program."

Then came another perspective-resetting realization: the students served by SPP are not just students. They are full human beings, with complex challenges and countless barriers. Gretchen, associate dean of general education with an educational and professional background in health sciences and leadership, named these disadvantages and barriers one by one: lack of affordable transportation, child care, health crises, disabilities, food insecurity, and the list goes on. Recognizing these challenges motivates the team to use their program and their classrooms as "a powerful equalizer, capable of removing the disadvantages that students might face in other contexts," as Rose expressed. But students don't just interface with the program, so a range of supports engaging various stakeholders also has to be in place to "get those things out of the way so they can focus on their learning," Gretchen said. And they did help get those things out of the way by bringing in something else—collegewide student support services that operate holistically with every student and their possible struggles in mind. These services include emergency funding, disability services, counseling services, food pantries, and an early alert system for communicating those student needs. Gretchen described the team's mentality: "We'll figure out what it is that they can't get, so that they have the tools they need to get started on their learning without delay. We just do all of the things that try, if life gets in the way, how do we just help you with that? Now focus on classes or focus on your learning."

This collective commitment not only helps remove barriers but also fuels the engagement of a larger support system to bolster students' learning through robust, collegewide supports, such as a tutoring system, career counseling, and other services. While these resources are common sights at many large institutions, minoritized students like those served by SPP do not always utilize them or are not even aware in the first place. So the team takes a different approach, Peter explained: "There's no sink or swim in this group, it's all high, high levels of support." What they ended up doing is embedding these services early on and creating particular time points within the students' first semester to "create an intentional touch base throughout as needed," according to Rose. In the same vein, the team has pivotal supports and opportunities related to students' transfer or career development intentionally placed at strategic points. For instance, the team taps into prescheduled industry partners' meetings and speed-hiring events as a way for students to secure internships or graduates to obtain jobs, along with coaching to prepare them for those events. "All those things along the way are just awesome wins that we've picked up by having great partners and trying to be intentional along the way," Peter further explained.

## TAKING AWAY THE NO'S

*If you are not gonna do this [transfer partnership], give me reasons why you're not going to do this and I'm going to take away every single one of those reasons over our period of years. Yeah, it's been a long time coming, but I think ultimately, it's for the students. If you keep the vision in mind, it becomes a lot easier, because ultimately the students are the ones that will benefit from all that work.*

—Steven

Speaking of partners and partnerships, the most inspiring and yet the most poignant part of the SPP story is its journey of building partnerships, especially transfer. It is a journey of visioning and doing something even when being told it's impossible. It is inspiring because the team moved mountains for the sake of creating a bright and broad future for their students. It is poignant because no student-centered partnership work should have involved so many no's and roadblocks. Years later, Steven still spoke of that journey with a deep resolve underlined by a hint of cynicism: "If you are not gonna do this [partnership], give me reasons why you're not going to do this and I'm going to take away every single one of those reasons over our period of years. Yeah, it's been a long time coming, but I think ultimately, it's for the students. If you keep the vision in mind, it becomes a lot easier, because ultimately the students are the ones that will benefit from all that work."

When Steven and Peter conceived the SPP in 2012, the college had no associate degree in the sciences with a strong research component. There was a semester or two that students could transfer from the college to a university, but not an integrated, seamless associate program that robustly prepared students for either transfer or employment. That's how the team envisioned the program, out of next to nothing in the local context. Because it was so rare at the time to have a program like this on a technical college campus, the team initially received pushback from within and beyond MTC—not because it wasn't a good idea, but because of statewide policies and requirements at the time that imposed a lot of restrictions on such a program.

But the team didn't give up; it engaged in what Peter described as a backward and forward design: "We kind of built it backward, saying, if we want to do research, what is the program that we would have to build to make research make sense here at MTC? Not something that's just tacked on, but really something that's part of a whole two-year experience. Because then it fits in our model as a college, as a two-year degree that could lead to employment or could lead to transfer." They also think forward, from questions like, "What types of roles are out there right now? And what are the skills that are needed? How do we then package that into this two-year type of program?" Gretchen recalled. This broad visioning resonated with institutional leadership, which Peter described as supportive in "keeping our idea for a program that featured research and transfer opportunities alive and actually kept true to the college's mission." The team eventually made the program possible—an *and* pathway instead of an *or* pathway that occurred in close response to the larger institutional and industry priorities. As Peter summed up: "What we came up with ultimately in the end was much better than anything I ever dreamed of, because it wasn't just a research opportunity that students could choose to be part of. It was a whole experience—beginning to end—where we built research in at multiple points, and it really became a part of a whole."

Indeed, SPP is guided by a holistic, future-oriented vision. Not limited by what's narrowly defined as a vocational education, it is a vision of lifelong learning and developing the whole person and what they are capable of, both now and down the road in students' life journeys. Steven shared how this vision is threaded into all facets of the SPP: "It just can't be, you're gonna learn to skill and job out. You need to also develop human skills. How do you communicate with another person in a respectful manner? How do you interact with people? How do you collaborate? Things like that. To contextualize it to a broader picture, having it be based on a person rather than just a sprocket in the machine."

From that vision, the team was all about making curricula fully align with transfer and industry partners—starting with core skills that transcend and are relevant to all parties. As a telling example, when Mary was writing some of the courses for the SPP, alignment with both transfer and industry partners was a key part of that process. She shared with me the complexities and challenges of developing organic chemistry courses that would serve both students interested in transfer and those who would be directly entering the workforce: "As a transfer course, there's pretty much a set list of topics that you go to any of the [state universities], they're going to teach pretty much the exact same thing in Organic I and Organic II, and I have to make sure I'm following that exactly. But not all of our students are going to be transferring. So how do I make sure I get those students skills for the workforce and just to work in a lab?" Creating the courses with transfer in mind was doable since there were structured concepts, content, and outcomes. However, coupling that with industry expectations and needs was a whole other task. So Mary approached industry partners to find out what kinds of skills they wanted to see in students coming out of the SPP. She then set about tackling the varying educational and professional goals of her students, along with the necessary knowledge and skills, all in one set of courses. Adding these extra steps or scenarios to the traditional labs ensured that SPP curricula and courses capture core skills that are broadly meaningful to all parties involved.

Until then, the SPP team had accomplished a rare and extraordinary feat, having developed a program that would meet both university needs and the needs of employers. But that was only the beginning. Then it was about getting transfer and industry partners onboard. And here began all of the proving to do. First and most challenging were the universities. As an obvious first choice, the team approached a state public university in the same town, just twenty minutes away. And they were met with a polite, nonetheless flat-out no: "We don't see this happening," Peter recalled. So, the team hit the road to visit with various other potential partners. They finally made headway with another university, which had a science department that exuded a less rigid and traditional academic structure and culture. This university was more responsive, but it wasn't smooth sailing either. There was an initial hesitation to view MTC's classes as equivalent to theirs, Peter recalled. The team did not give up; it requested many more meetings to review the program line by line. And the team had to prove more, as Peter described: "We showed them our labs, they actually came and viewed our labs. We said, 'We are committed to offering an equivalent learning experience to what your students get, tell us where we're missing something, tell us what we would need to do.' What they found was that we were doing just fine. Our classes were equivalent. Our students were learning well, our technology or labs were all up to snuff. There really was nothing that was missing." When asked why the second university was responsive to their persistent requests, Peter shook his head when sharing the unfortunate tactic that they had to use—have team members with PhDs represent the team: "I think university faculty viewed us closer to colleagues. Then they unfortunately viewed less of some of our colleagues who didn't have a PhD in science."

Concurrently working with industry partners during that time period also paid off. Although the team experienced some hurdles with industry partners, they were nothing like what it had to overcome with the universities. By that time, the SPP already had eight industry partners onboard. Then a synergistic opportunity came along that helped advance the program's transfer vision into reality. MTC held an event inviting local companies and organizations to a two-day brainstorming session to vet new programs that were being developed by the college, so as to help align them with core industry competencies and standards. The team jumped at this opportunity and invited potential university partners along. Seeing the vibrancy, appeal, and potential of the program, the university with which the team was already in conversation proceeded with the transfer partnership. "We then made a lot of headway, getting our classes approved for transfer [to this university]," Peter said. The team then went back to the local university that it first approached, just to show them the "credibility" of what it was offering and again asked the institution to participate, and ultimately, it did.

Listening to all this, I couldn't help but think of the many transfer-aspiring students from my other research, like Kanda in my book *On My Own*, where there was not a single public transfer option for certain programs that the students wanted.[1] As a result, they had to defer transfer since the other private options were simply out of their financial reach. Had the students had access to programs like the SPP that the team fought so hard to bring to fruition? When I shared with Peter my sentiments, he admitted that he and his team felt some complicated emotions, like the pride they had to swallow, even though they had a strong desire to show off to the local university when they got the first partnership. As much as they wanted to flaunt, "Hey, we are as good," and maintain a program partnership only with the first university that was willing to give them a glance, deep down they knew "that wasn't right, and that wasn't the right way for students," Peter adamantly concluded. The local university did eventually come around, and that partnership has also grown and flourished, with additional program partnerships and university leadership openly praising students that come from the SPP.

Although these hard-won relationships are significant accomplishments to celebrate, it really should not be how transfer partnerships work. When I asked Steven what were the biggest hurdles that the SPP had to overcome, for the first time in our multiple interviews did I hear a less upbeat Steven, speaking with a hint of sadness and defeat in his tone: "That we were not good enough. That, somehow, our students were not good enough. That still exists and it still just bothers me. There's history and things like that. Still, it's like, I don't know, it's almost like we're all in the same ship paddling opposite directions, whereas if we all could get in the same direction and try to remove some of these biases."

## A MARATHON AND SPRINTS AT THE SAME TIME

*So, always looking at the bigger picture and the goal. What is your goal? If our goal is to serve our students, are we meeting that goal with this path?*

—ROSE

The SPP innovation didn't happen because of the pandemic; it predated 2020, but it withstood the test of COVID-19 and was renewed with an even deeper sense of commitment. All the while, the team also navigated the pandemic journey within the larger personal, professional, and institutional contexts that were at times filled with challenges and tensions. First, like many of the educators in this book, the team also experienced significant burnout that required serious pausing, reflecting, and addressing by the institution. Invariably across my interviews, everyone talked about burnout—something that one couldn't tell having just watched their knockout performances in the classroom or during advising sessions, but something nonetheless so real. As Eve put it, "It is like we're expected to run a marathon and do sprints at the same time. It's kind of impossible. Everyone just expects, 'OK, you've got to do it. You just have to grit your teeth and get through it.'" Even for this most vigorous group of innovators, "there's not a lot of energy left over for all of these cool new things that we could implement," Mary said.

Doing the impossible led to mental health struggles for instructors and students alike—something that Eve identified as one of the biggest challenges: "Mental health struggles is one of the big trends we're seeing. A lot of students are struggling and are coming to us, saying, 'Hey, I'm having anxiety issues. I'm struggling at home with this.'… Honestly, that's where I struggle the most and that's where I start to feel burnout. I'm always happy to meet with them, like mentoring SPP students is one of my favorite parts, but I just I feel like it just starts to, when you're helping them through some really terrible things sometimes, I just feel burnout emotionally, mentally." Currently, the college (and most institutions, for that matter) does not offer training for faculty to support student mental health, and for Eve, that's a missed opportunity: "We're the first people students come to just because we're with them in class. That's one of the places where we're lacking support, which is draining us because we're kind of taking on that emotional burden from a lot of our students, and we're not really seeing the support from the college and, 'Hey, well here's some mental health training. Here's some personal counseling training.'" Eve provided feedback to the college's faculty development unit to "get some more training on mental health and personal counseling and supporting students" in the hope that mental health support and professional development get built into the larger institutional support structure, where holistic health and well-being are a part of faculty's repertoire to support students without sacrificing their own.

Another complicating part of the pandemic struggles were collegewide, rapid adjustments, such as implementing eight-week terms. As an example of accelerated terms that started to gain traction at many community and technical colleges in recent years, the eight-week model was already announced in July 2018 at MTC, with implementation taking place in the summer of 2020.[2] Given the timing, this model seemed appealing in terms of minimizing disruptions. Based on the experiences of the SPP faculty, it did not work well for students, as it created a mismatch between the state-aligned curricula and the pace and amount of space needed to process the content. Grappling with the potential pitfalls of what appears to be a budding institutional innovation, SPP members expressed their desire for robust evidence and thoughtful conversations to inform institutional decisions. Samantha further raised the equity implications of such efforts:

> I think we have some students that are fine with it [eight weeks] and would be fine in any format. We also have a lot of students for whom it's a struggle—they're trying to balance family, and job, and kids, and school…. The doors now have been open to have those conversations, and let's see what we can do. What's going to be best? Again, it's not necessarily that no students benefit from eight weeks. Some do, but some don't, and let's, if we're gonna talk about being equitable for our students; that's a big deal to the college, then let's actually be equitable. And what does that look like?

Through email conversations long after my visit, I learned that, over the course of many months, SPP's department collaborated with several other academic departments to review course success, student experiences, and downward trends of enrollments and upward trends of drops. Based on this holistic analysis grounded in evidence, they brought forward a formal request—which was granted by the college—for the SPP courses, along with other science courses, to return to the sixteen-week model. While the long-term impacts of accelerated semester models that continue at many places for different programs and students are yet to be learned, SPP's experimentation with the eight-week terms may feel more like both a marathon and sprints, rather than the intended short sprints with revitalizing breaks in between. More important, it illuminates how vital it is to guide change and innovation—especially the kinds that deeply affect teaching and learning—with transparency, invitations for input, and ultimately sound, equity-guided rationales supported by high-quality data.

## THE WORK IS ON US

*It's the work on us. And not saying that the students have to come to us. It doesn't matter if they come to us prepared or not prepared. We've got to find ways to get them there, and then keep them moving forward.*

—GRETCHEN

Finally, although SPP's success even during a global pandemic can't be decoupled from leadership practices that embody trust and flexibility, the team admitted to some larger looming challenges within the institutional culture and leadership: massive burnout, faculty turnover, early retirement, and other issues. Further, there will always be threats to newer programs such as SPP as the institution navigates budgets, competing priorities, leadership turnover, and legislative battles that often get in the way of educational innovations. "I fear politics because politics don't usually use logic to make decisions," Steven put poignantly. But he also believes that there is enough support behind their program at the institution, especially in light of the fact that SPP's success is situated within a slow but transformative institutional evolution.

Gretchen provided me with additional insights into this institutional journey. I had the opportunity to meet her on a peaceful Friday morning at the campus coffee shop. While the ambience was serene, Gretchen was already caught up grappling with a crisis in the health program on a different campus. Throughout our conversation, she remained focused and attentive, though keeping a watchful eye on her phone and email as the emergency unfolded. Her mantra for providing optimal support was clear: "Address the questions that students didn't even know to ask and get rid of things that are barriers out of the way."

Gretchen shared with me their team's evolving vision of SPP through the years, set against the backdrop of the larger national reform agenda for community colleges, notably starting with the Achieving the Dream network the college joined around 2010, and the Guided Pathways framework it adopted a few years later. She pointed to the focus on improving student success, recounting how leadership at the time was already shifting the perspective and responsibility from the student to the college: "It just helped all of us start to think about and figure out: What does that mean? And how does it change how we do our work? What are the services that we provide?" This meant looking at the "student services side of things," like student orientation, advising, involvement and activities, and getting information out. As the work has continued to unfold, the college has become much more in tune with students' ever-shifting needs. As Gretchen stated:

> Pre-pandemic certainly, we saw a lot of change with mental health concerns. We have many students of socioeconomic disadvantages. Our community was starting to grow to have more diversity and more students of color. How are we adjusting and adapting to all of those changing needs? Certainly, then pandemic, the world shifted. We had to adapt, and now even post-pandemic-ish, how were we adapting to the students who were isolated for so many years? Who may or may not know the technology that we are now using because it's much more flexible, accessible?

The Achieving the Dream network and later the Guided Pathways reform model have helped the college start those shifts, in both operation and perspective, toward transforming support structures to create more equitable experiences and outcomes for students. And that institutional cultural evolution is an integral context for understanding SPP's journey. But these operational changes and adaptations don't always point to clear insights that inform educators working on the ground about how to carry out daily, incremental change that leads to broader impact. Gretchen shared that this challenge is now widely recognized at MTC as it continues to seek answers to questions that define the essential experience of the institution: "What is our teaching, and how are we facilitating learning in a classroom?" And this all sets up SPP as a rare and shining example that helps further unpack these critical spaces of teaching, learning, and student support. It involves the entire college engaging innovation as part of the institutional culture, and in ways that both are systematic and place students and equity at the core of the ordinary everyday work.

Gretchen agreed. Coming back to her own mantra for the optimal types of supports, an instructor or an advisor or anyone else that the student encounters on campus—she pointed to the coffee shop's cashier—would have to do what the SPP embodies: caring and knowing the students' goals and contexts enough to give them what they need and remove barriers that they don't have to deal with: "It's the work on us. And not saying that the students have to come to us. It doesn't matter if they come to us prepared or not prepared. We've got to find ways to get them there, and then keep them moving forward."

Toward the end of my visit, I had the opportunity to observe the semi-annual meeting of the SPP advisory committee, which consisted of the core team and industry and university partners. This venue provided student data and various moments for pivotal discussions about the program's direction and vitality. As I followed along, I felt the pride that members took in naming each student individually, emphasizing each one's personal connections and accomplishments. I resonated with the honest discussion of perennial challenges, such as how to ensure that students fully understand the prospects of transferring versus seeking employment immediately. I was energized by the unwavering emphasis on making impactful opportunities accessible for all students. I marveled at the commitment and action—shared by industry partners and educators alike—toward developing students into well-rounded, equity-minded citizens, far beyond technical skills training. In a word, I witnessed how a group of dedicated educators and their partners wove the threads of student empowerment, equity, and limitless possibilities into the fabric of SPP's future.

To this day, as I pour words onto pages, my heart is still bursting with inspiration, reflexivity, joy, and an utter sense of awe. The SPP deserves another whole venue to do it full justice, but the gist of why it leads as an innovation is that its core members have been ahead of the times and their students' needs, exemplifying the innovator mindset, as Eve put it: "You have to be able to adapt to innovate, to come up with new ways because student needs are always changing, and we have to be able to meet those needs. We always have to come up with a new way; we can't just stick to the tried and true."

Having learned from the many rich program documents, spoken at length with each of the team members, and seen all of them in action over and again, I know this remarkable innovation called the SPP didn't happen randomly or easily; it's dedication, persistence, teamwork, leadership support, and everyone's willingness to go out of their way to make what seems impossible possible for their students. It is one of the most remarkable educational innovations in the landscape of community and technical college education as well as transfer. And it should be treasured as such.

## QUESTIONS FOR REFLECTION

- What are the key highlights or ideas of the SPP that stand out to you?
- In what ways does the SPP challenge your preconceptions or assumptions about the role of technical education?
- How does the SPP challenge traditional notions of STEM education?

- Do any specific teaching and student support approaches employed by SPP resonate with you? How can you incorporate similar strategies into your own practices?
- Reflecting on SPP's journey of building partnerships, what lessons can be learned about overcoming obstacles and persisting in the pursuit of equity and innovation? How can these lessons be applied to other educational initiatives?
- Considering the role of mentors within the SPP, how might mentorship be integrated more intentionally in other educational contexts?
- How does the SPP balance the development of technical and academic skills with the cultivation of essential human skills? How might this integrated approach reshape the future of STEM education and workforce readiness?
- How does SPP's comprehensive support structure address the complex needs and challenges that students face beyond the classroom? What can other institutions learn from this model to enhance equitable student support services?
- How does SPP's collaborative approach promote equitable opportunities for students? What innovative possibilities arise from forging closer relationships between educational institutions and industry partners to create broadened pathways for underrepresented students?
- How does the success of the SPP challenge your perceptions of what can be achieved through internal budgetary resources and grassroots initiatives to advance equity in education? How might you advocate for similar support and investment in transformative programs within your own institution?
- If given the chance to redesign the SPP from scratch, what alternative models or approaches would you consider to ensure that students have equitable access to the program? How might you design the program so that it proactively addresses systemic barriers and promotes inclusive practices?

# A Path Forward

## Advancing Equity-Driven
## Change and Innovation

*We always had innovation and inspiration and transformation as part of our
mantra. And adding collaboration, but adding really how we are purposefully
being inclusive? There are so many variables in our students' lives and in the
communities within that we serve—How are we honoring that diversity within
the community and then building the best inroads to what they need next?*

—HELEN, VICE PRESIDENT, MIDWESTERN STATE ASSOCIATION OF COLLEGES

THIS BOOK WAS researched and written during a global pandemic, when
higher education has been presented with what appears to be a dire
future. Indeed, as so much media and so many of my participants cautioned, higher education is at a critical juncture, challenged by plummet-
ing enrollment coupled with a declining interest in college among high
school graduates.[1] Not to even mention long-existing and amplified inequities baked into education and society well before the pandemic. Wade,
president of Nova Technical College, reflected on the most pressing issues
that he hopes to seek answers for about how colleges like his recover from

the pandemic: "How do students make postsecondary decisions, and how has their decision-making process evolved and changed? How can we best structure the educational experience to meet whatever those needs are? That's a heavy lift, and what organizational structures fit that best? These are the questions that keep rolling around in my head. And when we make those decisions as an organization deliberately, knowing that we may not meet the needs of some students and are we OK with that?"

Wade's preoccupation with these questions is both a concern for many and a motivation that drove the evolving change and innovation described in this book that turned out to brighten even my darkest days of the past few years. These efforts evolve to be closer and closer to a vision that has the potential to resolve Wade's and other leaders' equity concerns. Steph, administrative chair of general education at Parkfield Technical College and an expert in universal design for learning (UDL), captured this vision metaphorically: "It has become more pronounced to me that UDL at every level of education is really important. That doesn't limit itself to just the way that we design an individual course or the way we design a program, or the methods by which we teach our classes. I really think that UDL has to really take a look at the pathways, the ramps. We have to meet students where they are and provide them the resources to get what they need to get to where they want to be."

As a whole, these innovative feats, as systematic as the Science Pathway Program (SPP) or as incremental as Renee's messaging of care, are a testament to community and technical colleges' historic propensity to change and innovate. Of no less importance, they unravel both the urgency and some of the most pressing challenges for enacting equity-driven educational innovations in contemporary times. Most prominently, though, they shine a light on generative ways to address both pandemic-imposed challenges and enduring equity gaps. In this final chapter, I first offer a discussion of the key challenges and lessons learned as revealed by the collective insights of my participants. These are nuanced and complex issues that, if confronted and thoughtfully tackled, present opportunities for enacting lasting change. Based on this discussion and with a forward gaze, I lay out a blueprint that fuses innovation and equity as one charge to address the deepest realities and inequities of students and institutions alike.

## CHALLENGES AHEAD: RECENTERING EQUITY FROM WITHIN AND WITHOUT

I stressed earlier in this book, and I want to be clear again, long before the pandemic, there was no shortage of educational innovations on the community and technical college scene. Over the past few decades, this sector has undergone a number of impactful reform efforts that set the stage for many of the changes and innovations that I have documented. One of the most prominent ones, the Achieving the Dream network, started in 2004 to bring colleges together and support them in their shared efforts to tackle data collection and data use in community colleges to bolster student success.[2] Several years later, Guided Pathways gained traction as an empirically based framework that proposed a series of shifts and reforms aimed at restructuring community colleges and their programs and supports to improve student outcomes.[3] These are the primary support networks or reform processes that about two-thirds of my interviewees' institutions participated in or adopted over the years. As large reform efforts, both have done unparalleled work in advancing community and technical college education on multiple fronts. To name two of the most noteworthy, for one, they have helped many colleges start to not only move from access to successful outcomes, but more important, to reconceptualize the structural foundation of how students move through the institution toward their goals. For another, many institutions involved in these reforms made headway in making continuous improvements and bringing more empirical evidence, often through routine administrative data accessible to the college, to the discussions and initiatives about student success. In brief, they helped establish much of the structural foundation and perspective shifts for the colleges to engage in efforts toward reaching equity goals. Yet the trials, errors, and triumphs of the practitioners I describe in this book show that the solutions to persistent inequities remain elusive even within large reforms that embrace equity goals. My participants offered intensely honest and nuanced insights into three different but interrelated challenges.

The first is the equity-oblivious mentality that I described in the introduction to this book, even with the sincerest intentions. It means while the word "equity" may be written or spoken somewhere, it somehow loses its meaning in translation when it's conflated with other constructs like access or success, or more often than not, when equity is treated as an afterthought rather than being purposefully woven into all facets of change, especially from the very early stages of conceptualization. As many practitioners in my book have pointed out, while "equity" had been a key word for many of the institutional initiatives that they participated in or were aware of, the pandemic really opened their eyes, for the first time, to the equity gaps that had always been there, right across all the spaces in which they operate. This clearly amplifies the urgency to change the lens through which we view and enact change with intended equity goals in mind.[4] Estela Bensimon and colleagues at the University of Southern California's Center for Urban Education illuminate how to accomplish that with the concept of equity-mindedness, which speaks to a mindset shift that requires institutions and educators to take responsibility for and address inequities.[5] Lorenzo Baber, Eboni Zamani-Gallaher, Tamara Stevenson, and Jeff Porter particularly propose a change in the role of community colleges toward equity-centeredness.[6] This critical lens challenges these institutions to interrogate data, practices, and resources toward supporting, scaling, and sustaining equity.

A second, related challenge is the stubborn fact that inequities reside everywhere, across all educational spaces and structures. This means at least two big realities that I must name. To begin with, student inequities exist and can be reinforced everywhere, from admissions policies to grading practices, from program structures to support services, from teaching practices to financial aid award processes, and much more. Working across these innumerable spaces, my participants showed that, without letting equity into these spaces as the guiding light for everything we do, no amount of change in structures and operations can solve the disparities that we set out to alleviate. In addition, inequities are an inherent part of the lived challenges, struggles, and constraints for those working on the ground to enact change—practitioners, leaders, and institutional partners alike—from institutional resources to capacity issues, from professional development to partnership building, and from institutional culture to accountability structures, among others. These inequities are compounded in community colleges as racialized organizations, further marginalizing these institutions and the students that enroll there, as Heather McCambly and colleagues argued.[7] Without naming and working toward eradicating such inequities, we will continue to work in vain, or even worse, carry those unresolved inequities over into student work, missing the mark on serving and supporting those whom we purport to serve and support.

A third interlacing challenge is the dominant institutional culture and leadership model that positions equity work in precarious ways. Specifically, an institutional culture without sufficient care and trust doesn't empower its people to engage in and enact equity work, but instead it ends up with those on the ground having their hands tied, ultimately undermining such efforts. This can make change that centers equity, or any change for that matter, replete with obstacles if not completely stalled, as Adrianna Kezar points out in her work on change in higher education.[8] Add in leadership priorities and commitment to equity shifting due to increasing college leader turnover, making it even more difficult to create any consistent and impactful headway. And this is to be even further complicated by the larger political environments in several states that restrict institutions from carrying out many of the emergent equity initiatives, along with a recent historic Supreme Court ruling ending affirmative action in college admissions, a decision that will have lasting impacts on racial equity. While these larger issues of politics, priorities, and culture are yet to play out in major ways over the next few years, the truth of the matter is that individual educators can't be left with little agency, understanding, and clear know-how to engage in equity-driven change that makes a positive difference in the lives of the students who come through their doors every day. At the intersection of these huge equity challenges came one of my biggest learnings from the participants and writing this book. It is the transformational power of turning the everyday ordinary educational spaces into something extraordinary for a student from a minoritized background. It requires us to interrogate our "discretionary spaces," a term coined by Deborah Loewenberg Ball, where educators have the authority and power to make decisions and enact change to remove inequities among students.[9]

The countless reflections and stories of change and innovation in this book, including those seemingly nonconsequential and yet pivotal moments and windows for action and change, all compel us to intentionally and holistically recognize these spaces as opportunities for initiating and sustaining equity-driven innovation. Carl, dean of science, technology, engineering, and mathematics (STEM) at Inland Community College, brought these thoughts to light, along with a pressing question for us all moving forward: "So the pandemic has taught us to be flexible, has taught us to be innovative, it's taught us to be equitable. How do we continue to do that as we begin to transition from the pandemic? And does that transition ever happen?"

## A PATH FORWARD

I now present a path toward enacting equity-driven change and innovation in community and technical colleges, as illustrated in figure 8.1. It results from my culminating analysis of this entire study and in conversation with the evolving landscape of practice and research pertaining to these institutions. Situated within student and institutional realities and

**FIGURE 8.1**   Path toward enacting equity-driven educational change and innovation: Six imperatives

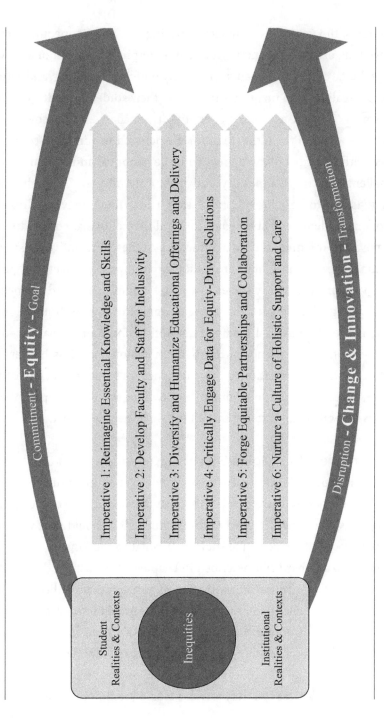

Commitment – **Equity** – Goal

Imperative 1: Reimagine Essential Knowledge and Skills

Imperative 2: Develop Faculty and Staff for Inclusivity

Imperative 3: Diversify and Humanize Educational Offerings and Delivery

Imperative 4: Critically Engage Data for Equity-Driven Solutions

Imperative 5: Forge Equitable Partnerships and Collaboration

Imperative 6: Nurture a Culture of Holistic Support and Care

Disruption – **Change & Innovation** – Transformation

Student Realities & Contexts

Inequities

Institutional Realities & Contexts

contexts, the key motivating factor driving this path is inequities that have long existed. This nonnegotiable centerpiece came out of a pervasive theme of the participants reflectively noticing, honoring, and acting on the realities and inequities that affect their students, institutions, or partners. They are at the core of equity-driven change and innovation—both its *why* and the ultimate *so-what*. Anchored within these contexts, there are six imperatives aligned with the historical and contemporary challenges facing community and technical colleges. Although there may appear to be a logical progression across them, they will have to work in tandem to position educators and their efforts as equity-driven, innovation-oriented, and interconnected. At these imperatives' juxtaposition is the shining light where equity and innovation converge to guide the path forward. Equity serves as a goal, a commitment, and an anchor underlying all the processes leading to impactful change. Innovation is exemplified by the dual theme of disruption and transformation—disruption of mindsets and practices that have long acted as barriers to equity, and transformation in the experiences of students and educators alike, especially those to whom an equity debt is owed. I unpack these ideas in more detail through each of the six imperatives next.

## Imperative 1: Reimagine Essential Knowledge and Skills

The first imperative is to revisit, update, or develop the institutional vision of the essential knowledge and skills for students, and align curricula and programs accordingly. Any educational innovation should start with the core purpose—to educate the students. Similar to the forward and backward thinking that Peter described in chapter 7, the post-pandemic education, industry, and society writ large require a reexamination of what it means to be college-educated and what essential knowledge and skills are really needed, not from the past—what's always been done—but future oriented. Findings from this book (chapters 2, 3, and 7) and recent research by Matthew Hora and colleagues have shown that technical or "hard" skills are only a piece of a truly forward-looking community and technical education.[10] Knowledge and competencies that build the whole person—critical thinking, communication, collaboration, problem-solving, and especially timely and relevant, how to practice all that with diversity, equity, and inclusivity as a guiding light—allow students to engage productively and meaningfully across holistic domains of their lives and best align with the needs and wants of both industry and universities. In particular, for equity to truly take hold, it should not only be reflected within the institution and its faculty, staff, and leaders, but also be evident in the student body and mindsets. And with that forward thinking comes the backward design to revitalize existing curricula and programs accordingly.

In chapter 2, I described some promising practices toward making curricula and course requirements more meaningful and relevant to students' lives, cultures, and other important contexts. More than ever, it is critical for faculty and academic leaders to interrogate whether their program and course offerings are indeed preparing their students with truly transferrable and transformative competencies for an ever more diverse and complex future in their education and careers.

## Imperative 2: Develop Faculty and Staff for Inclusivity

The second imperative is faculty and staff development toward inclusive student learning and support. Any innovative professional development that promotes equitable and inclusive practices must begin with decentering whiteness and decolonizing curricula and student support, as discussed in chapters 2 and 3. This means rethinking course structures and policies, academic supports, and student services to gauge who is being served—and who is not—and deconstructing norms in ways that actually bolster student success. Also, any development should help faculty and staff cultivate high levels of inclusion and coordination across the college in ways that focus on students as whole persons throughout their college journeys.

Another key facet of faculty and staff development is to integrate critical and reflective data use that goes beyond merely presenting information on student outcomes, as we saw in chapter 5. It is about creating a better understanding of the students coming through the door, identifying barriers, and leaving with concrete action toward removing them. However, development must also model inclusivity for engaging and empowering faculty and staff as equal partners if there is to be action, and ultimately advancement of equity work.

## Imperative 3: Diversify and Humanize Educational Offerings and Delivery

Closely related, the third imperative is to identify diverse and inclusive ways to deliver education that humanizes pedagogy and technology. This imperative reflects and resonates with the broader notion of humanizing higher education as advanced by Joy Gaston Gayles, which emphasizes thoughtful and intentional educational approaches and innovations that extend care and responsibility, especially to those who have been historically marginalized.[11] The rising challenges in instructional modality and scheduling (chapter 7) make it crucial to seek solutions that optimally serve a diverse student body with ever more diverse needs, goals, and learning styles. Regardless of their own preferences, my participants all came to acknowledge the necessity of diversifying instructional delivery modes (like online-synchronous, online-asynchronous, hybrid, blended, and hyflex[12]), academic terms (through accelerated formats such as eight-week courses), and scheduling options (ranging from on-campus or online remote learning to staggered start or year-round). The need to experiment with these options is salient, given their potential equity implications for students who can't afford to come to campus every day because of employment, caretaking, parenting, or lack of stable, consistent transportation. Yet I want to caution that a naive adoption of these approaches solely based on perceived expediency and access may not align with what students actually need to succeed. These new ways of delivering education need much more deliberate planning, thoughtful implementation, and timely applied research and data to gauge their efficacy and equity.

And precisely because of these inequities, this domain of innovation not only means extending diverse options, but more important, centering approaches that humanize pedagogy and the use of technology to ensure richly meaningful experiences that are responsive to students' realities instead of merely access, with lots of unresolved struggles and chaos. My book shows that this can be achieved even in a remote or hybrid model when it is ultimately about building communities that integrate access, clarity, order, and support. Regardless of technology and course structures, it is also vital to humanize pedagogy, guided by asset-based and trauma-informed lenses and facilitated by the hard work of decentering whiteness—that is, moving away from characterizing white middle-class norms as the only, dominant, and best way to teach, learn, and support students.

## Imperative 4: Critically Engage Data for Equity-Driven Solutions

Fourth, it is vital to generate and use data in reflective and action-oriented ways for identifying persistent equity blind spots and guiding equity-driven decisions and innovative solutions. A key premise for innovation in this domain is interrogating what counts as robust evidence and who has the power. As chapters 2, 3, and 4 showed, there are human-centered, experiential aspects of student learning and experiences, faculty teaching and support, and advisor and counselor interactions with students that can truly make a difference. Yet the gathering of such data and using them as a robust part of the culture of evidence is currently limited and should be elevated. Also, this book reveals pervasive power issues as reflected in the limited data use toward institutional action and adjustments. To bring this all into concert together, leadership must create opportunities and empower collaboration among administration, institutional researchers, faculty, and staff.

To facilitate implementation, equity-guided use of data should start with constructing and deconstructing the holistic college experience within the contexts of student progress through various academic, administrative, and other milestones or transitions, which helps illuminate spots where students struggle (or not). It should then be followed by a critical contextualization of data within structural supports or barriers to help identify points of intervention, course correction, and revision of the support types and structures. Although engaging in data disaggregation is an important part of these processes, it is not about which student groups didn't perform well, but rather how the structures and systems failed to support them. In the end, all of these should eventually lead to enacting equity-oriented change by using data to unclutter and holisticize—removing barriers and making relevant support part of students' holistic experience.

## Imperative 5: Forge Equitable Partnerships and Collaboration

Fifth, equitable partnership and collaboration models and approaches are essential to broadening education and career opportunities for minoritized students, whose postsecondary enrollment has consistently declined since COVID-19. To be more effective in recruiting and retaining students, especially those who have not been served well in the past, partnerships that prepare and empower students to secure meaningful careers and/or transfer to earn a bachelor's degree in a field of their passion in noncompeting ways are key. We have seen how the SPP does just that. Some of the more specific promising directions to try new partnerships include extending experiential learning opportunities to all students, not just those in technical education programs, to enrich students' knowledge and skills that they can carry over into a career, their communities, and/or their bachelor's degree programs post-transfer. Another direction is to reinvent liberal arts or general education studies so that they serve dual purposes, both as premajor transfer programs and as value to the local industries and economy.

For partnerships to be truly impactful, more than and before anything else, norms and power structures must be disrupted in such a way that power and authority are equitably distributed between community and technical college, university, and industry partners. With that in mind, an equity-guided partnership model should be characterized by a clear collaborative vision, a clear work plan, a clear commitment, and clear expectations of engagement. These ingredients must ensure that equity is reflected in the *what*, *why*, *who*, and *so-what* in everything that partners do, rather than doing everything that seems right and then thinking about equity implications. Otherwise, we run the risk of making superficial progress and ultimately perpetuating unintended consequences. An effective and powerful approach to realizing this vision is to ground everything within the perspective of how students, especially those from minorized backgrounds, navigate and are affected by the work of the partnership.

## Imperative 6: Nurture a Culture of Holistic Support and Care

Sixth, an institutional culture of holistic support and care is imperative for *everyone*. Behind every educational innovation to enact and every stubborn structure to dismantle, there are people full of their vulnerabilities, resilience, and potential for change. And in the same ways we strive to center students' holistic being, the educators' humanity must be factored as an inseparable part of the institutional fabric of support, especially at institutions that always operate with dwindling resources while striving for greater impact. Yet burnout and turnover have become especially pervasive since the pandemic.

To retain the highly talented and dedicated educators and leaders, a reconfiguring of institutional norms, structures, and supports is in order. This means viewing and treating educators as colleges' biggest assets through a culture and support system grounded in kindness, love, and trust. This translates into catching up with the evolving and elusive nature of educators' work in community and technical colleges, such as shifting instructional delivery that takes up additional work time and amplified mental health challenges among students; and responding with appreciation and flexibility. This also means striking a greater balance among educators' myriad roles and responsibilities—through facilitating and listening to honest conversations, along with training and support—to arrive at more equitable, innovative solutions without draining capacity. The same extends to institutional leaders, as we also see a looming leadership crisis that must be addressed, especially affecting women leaders and leaders of color who tend to carry the added weight of equity efforts. Not only are leaders the ones setting the tone for a caring institutional community, but they too require the same humanity and love as they make critical, real-time adjustments to inspire, engage, and support those around them.

## CONCLUDING THOUGHTS

I am fully aware that these imperatives for equity-driven, innovative efforts present trying challenges, especially amid continuously taxing social and political environments that always shape, and are responded to by, community and technical colleges. Helen, vice president of the Midwestern State Association of Colleges, captured the call to enact on equity and inclusivity, building on a long history of innovation in community and technical colleges, as follows: "We always had innovation and inspiration and transformation as part of our mantra. And adding collaboration, but adding really how we are purposefully being inclusive? There are so many variables in our students' lives and in the communities within that we serve. How are we honoring that diversity within the community and then building the best inroads to what they need next?"

Throughout this book, I have delineated my participants' experiential journeys toward growth and unlearning that touch upon one or more of these imperatives I have laid out in this chapter, as a practical way to help us think about what guides and centers us as individuals and a collective operating from day to day, project to project, and idea to idea. Although their trajectories, experiences, and stances differ, these educators invariably showed me that for community and technical colleges to thrive as engines of democracy and mobility, they must face the hard work of infusing equity into the change and innovation that they purport to engage with. The pandemic serves as both a magnifier and a microscope for some of the most enduring equity issues that beseech these institutions for new solutions, as both sites of opportunity and sites that can perpetuate inequity. They have risen to the occasion, reflectively albeit imperfectly, as sites of social responsiveness. Ultimately, though, this book is about the vast promise of community and technical colleges as sites of equity-driven educational change and innovation.

## QUESTIONS FOR REFLECTION

- In what ways can educators continue to structure impactful and equitable educational experiences that meet the evolving needs of all students in a post-pandemic education?
- How can educators use their own spaces of authority and power to remove barriers and inequities for students?
- In what ways can educators rethink essential knowledge and skills that develop the whole student toward success in all domains of their lives?
- How can educators embrace and value the process of unlearning and undoing in safe, empowering, and yet challenging spaces?
- What can be learned from past reform initiatives to inform future equity efforts in community and technical colleges?
- What policy measures can be implemented to address the systemic inequities embedded in community and technical college spaces and structures?
- How can policy makers and education leaders purposefully center equity work, including empowering others to participate in and enact such efforts?

- What structural changes are needed in education systems and policies to acknowledge and tap into the assets of individuals, students, communities, and partners involved in the educational ecosystem?
- How can institutional actors conceptualize and carry out equity-driven educational innovation, in light of institutional and student realities?

# Methodological Appendix

## WHAT I STUDIED AND WHY

As I recounted in the preface, I entered the larger research project behind this book inspired by the change, commitment, and compassion demonstrated by practitioner colleagues at community and technical colleges. But long before the pandemic, my professional and academic journey had allowed me to develop a deep affinity with the open access mission of these institutions and cultivate an equally deep commitment to the study and advancement of their leadership and practice. From my many research endeavors, often in collaboration with community and technical colleges, I have seen how these institutions open doors to minoritized populations while having unresolved, long-standing equity gaps. These realities and tensions have guided me in my own evolving equity-centered research agenda.

Although concerns around inequities weren't anything new, they became especially amplified in recent years, prompting community and technical colleges to confront them head-on. It is something that I personally witnessed through practitioner colleagues' efforts and struggles right around the onset of the COVID-19 global pandemic. It motivated me to launch a large-scale, fully integrated mixed methods research project later in 2020 to study changes and innovations at these institutions through an equity lens.[1] As an integral component of the larger project, from

October 2021 to March 2023, I interviewed 126 institutional stakehold-ers to understand how they engage with change and innovation during times of crisis while grappling with equity concerns. This book harnesses key findings from these interviews, presenting my participants' trials and errors, struggles and triumphs, along with the puzzles, tensions, and con-flicts that they continue to wrestle with. On many occasions, I also ana-lyzed written documents related to the interviewed participants—news media, policy documents, meeting and presentation documents, course and program catalogs, course syllabi, and other materials. This additional information, either through my own exploration or shared by my partici-pants, provided deeper and broader context to the interview findings.

## FROM WHOM, WHAT, AND WHERE I LEARNED

Overall, the interviews were rooted in a phenomenological approach, largely aligned with a hermeneutic tradition that focuses on the human experience as lived, through their life-world stories and open to mean-ing.[2] Adopting a largely interpretive lens, hermeneutic phenomenology is concerned with how someone is experiencing the world, as well as the iterative descriptions and interpretations associated with it.[3] This approach to interviewing is helpful in that it provides a window into the day-to-day lives and actions of the various stakeholders in their situ-ated cultural, social, and historical contexts.[4] In the case of this study, the shared phenomenon comprised community and technical college stakeholders' experiences and meaning-making around pandemic-induced change and innovation, as well as situating equity within their work. Hermeneutic phenomenology also captures the intensity of those experiences, such as the frustration, helplessness, love, hopefulness, and humanity as seen throughout the educators' narratives, lending richness and authenticity to the tangible challenges and promises these individu-als faced as they contended with pandemic-spurred change and innova-tion alongside pressing equity work.[5]

In the individual interviews, I first spent some time getting to know my participants' backgrounds and experiences leading up to and during their current role within their college context. Then I posed questions about their initial thoughts, feelings, and reactions to the pandemic when it first hit. For all participants, I asked about their experiences adjusting to the sudden disruptions of COVID-19 in light of their daily work, including any new or innovative approaches and efforts. Then depending on what they shared, I inquired about what worked well, what didn't, and what they learned from those experiences that would shape the future of their work (differently). During this part of the interview, sometimes without prompting and sometimes with my intentional follow-up questions, participants would reflect on and describe unintended consequences of the pandemic-spurred change and innovation, especially highlighting groups of students or other stakeholder groups not well served. This conversation often led participants to share their reflections on the disparities and equity gaps they had seen in their students and at their institutions predating and during the pandemic. Of no less importance, I asked my participants to share their own definitions, sensemaking, and tensions regarding equity and innovation, and what all these mean in their day-to-day work with students and colleagues. Throughout the interviews, I included multiple opportunities for participants to elaborate on the intensity and meaning of their experiences through concrete examples and stories. These interview questions were not prescriptive; rather, they served as a general road map that allowed me to adjust the questions and areas of discussion based on participants' own direction and the topics that they wished to cover.

While the bulk of the book draws from individual interviews, I also conducted case studies that are ideal for examining an institution, specific program, or initiative, including how individuals with varying intentions, motivations, and levels of power and influence interact with and respond to social or other external forces.[6] These case studies are grounded within data collected before, during, and after site visits, including observations, individual and focus group interviews, and documents that were publicly accessible or were made available by the participants. The interviews included the same types of questions described above, but often extended beyond those to touch upon what I noticed during my visits and observations. These multiple data sources bring to light authentic contexts and structures that help construct holistic portraits of the cases. I integrated case study findings with individual interview findings throughout various chapters, like chapters 1, 4, and 5. But it is important to note that I dedicated the entirety of chapter 7 to spotlighting a particular case, the Science Pathway Program (SPP). I chose this case for its richness in capturing the gist of an equity-centered innovation, as well as revealing the structural, political, and interpersonal complexities that were negotiated by the SPP.

Given the scope and focus of the book, I didn't highlight findings from the quantitative strand of the larger study. Nonetheless, they played a supporting role in various ways behind the scenes for this book. The quantitative strand entailed text mining techniques my team and I used to curate and analyze the large volume of policies, practices, and initiatives that have materialized since the pandemic, which are often described and included in various documents and media, primarily consisting of text data. Text mining techniques helped make full sense of the numerous policies, practices, and initiatives, especially the striking patterns of change and innovation and the focus on equity that have transpired since COVID-19. Some of these findings based on institutions from one of the Midwestern states in the study are reflected in figure 1.1 from chapter 1. Besides providing this broader picture, another important role of the quantitative strand was to guide the sampling and selection for the qualitative strand of the study, which I discuss next.

Although for this study, my unit of analysis is largely the individual educators instead of the institutions or the states, it is necessary to attend to the broader geographical and organizational contexts that situate their work. While a major part of this study took place in the

Midwest, my participants came from institutions across seven states in three larger geographical regions. I initiated the study in a Midwestern state with a robust technical education, along with institutions that have a broader range of functions including liberal arts education and baccalaureate transfer. This background makes this state context uniquely valuable, as it highlights technical colleges that tend to be overlooked while addressing enduring issues in the larger community college literature and practice. Following that same spirit to achieve broader relevance and diversity, I extended data collection to community and technical college practitioners—including a few university transfer partners—in other states, adding two more states in the Midwest, two in the South, and two in the West. These additional institutions range in geographical location and size, often with stakeholder and student populations that had greater racial and ethnic diversity. I chose these participants with hopes of seeing whether and how my findings would converge or diverge, and as reflected in the chapters, the themes coming out of these interviews are more often similarly synergistic than drastically different.

I went with the highest level of anonymity by not only deidentifying the participants and the institutions where they work, but also masking state names altogether to minimize the possibility of linking participants to their individual institutions and states, especially those who voiced concerns about institutional policies, leadership, or culture. Further, when describing participants' positions and roles within their institutions, I tweaked those titles with potentially identifying descriptors and words to be better aligned with more standard titles used to describe them in the field of higher education. These approaches helped make participants feel safe to share their experiences at their institutions and have both positive and challenging experiences reflected in the findings published in this book, without fear of identification or retribution. This also allows for a focus on the experiences and lessons learned within authentic institutional contexts rather than pointing fingers at specific colleges.

I used several methods to recruit participants. I began with purposeful sampling of stakeholders at all levels of the colleges, such as faculty, advisors, other student services staff, institutional researchers, directors, deans, vice presidents, and presidents.[7] The emerging text mining results initially guided this process by revealing prominent cases and individuals engaging in innovative efforts guided by equity, as well as specific topics and areas to explore more deeply. I also used a number of other ways to choose my participants and cases, as clearly, media outlets and communication venues are far from complete when covering some of the most salient stories. For example, as the study unfolded, I increasingly used snowballing, meaning that initial participants selected through media and text mining results were invited to suggest additional individuals who would be willing to share their experiences and insights related to the study.[8] Often, these participants were able to point me to their colleagues within and beyond their institutions and states, including some with the most innovative minds or practices that are far off the radar but critical to bring to light. Concurrently, I also tapped my own personal and professional networks nationally to identify individuals—often based on a history of knowing these people and seeing their work, impact, and leadership as applicable. In other instances, my interviews with some of the participants uncovered significant themes or directions that warranted further exploration, which led to follow-up interviews with the same participants, and in a few situations, a full case study that entailed both interviews and site visits. A total of 126 educators participated in one or more in-depth interviews.

In summary, 38.1 percent of my participants are faculty; 20.6 percent staff members in student services, learning support, or other roles; 18.3 percent administrators; and 13.5 percent executive leaders. In addition, 9.5 percent of my participants work in institutional research offices or similar functional areas. Although technically also staff, institutional researchers are a distinct group whose work is critical and yet undervalued and understudied, so I designated them as a separate group not only to highlight their significance, but also to reflect the attention they receive in chapter 4. In terms of gender and race, 53.2 percent of the participants identified as women and 34.8 percent are people of color. The vast majority are thirty-five years of age and older and come from a middle- to upper-middle-class background. Of the individuals I interviewed, 44.4 percent have a doctorate or professional degree. For additional information on the entire interview sample, see table A.1 at the end of this appendix.

The themes and arguments I present throughout this book are based on the interviews with all participants. In selecting data to report, it is not always feasible to include every single person, as much value as each interview brings to the study, especially when capturing an experience and core meanings through an interpretative lens.[9] I ended up choosing quotes and stories that are both salient and aligned with the overall themes that emerged.[10] Table A.2 at the end of this appendix provides further detailed background information on the seventy-three participants featured in the book, along with the chapters in which their stories and quotes appear.

## HOW I GATHERED DATA AND INFORMATION

I conducted the interviews either virtually or in person and site visits in person, depending on participant preference and proximity, and importantly, COVID-19 restrictions and guidelines. During the interviews, I asked a set of common questions described earlier, along with those tailored to the individuals and adapted to the flow of the conversation. Interviews averaged sixty minutes, but some lasted up to two hours. Participants were offered a $30 cash incentive, although many declined payment. Before, during, and/or after each interview and site visit, I also researched or requested additional contextual information like professional background, written correspondence, articles and media sources, and website information, along with any other relevant data that would add texture and richness to the stories and findings. In many cases, participants also willingly shared documents and resources such as syllabi, strategic plans, policy documents, book chapters, reports, catalogs, meeting and presentation documents, and on occasion, their own published works, which often gave valuable insights into the contexts and complexities underlying their experiences.

## HOW I MADE SENSE OF THE DATA

The interviews were recorded and transcribed. I then analyzed them iteratively through multiple levels of sensemaking and interpretation. Throughout data collection, I journaled and took extensive notes after the completion of each interview. During this process, I recorded and reflected on significant occurrences of facts, emotions, points of tension, interactions, and reactions.[11] This served as a preliminary sensemaking of the interviews and the participants' overall experiences. Also, I documented my own reactions, including unanswered questions and unexpected findings and learnings, as well as what might have been my assumptions and biases, and put them in conversation with all of my initial sensemaking.[12] Throughout this process, I often developed follow-up questions or requests for additional interviews or information to enrich and clarify preliminary findings that I would continue fleshing out during the next part of my analysis.

When working with the fully transcribed interviews, I immersed myself in the data, reading the transcripts and listening to the recordings numerous times. Within the interview transcripts, I annotated participants' key ideas through their own words, phrases, and statements. This facilitated an interpretive process engaging a dialectical interaction between my preliminary understanding and the meaning arising from the interview data.[13] Through multiple iterations of putting my reflective notes and emerging sensemaking in conversation with salient experiences and units of meaning as reflected in the written transcripts, I was able to move toward an ever richer and deeper understanding of the phenomenon from different perspectives, roles, and positions.[14] I also compiled textual descriptions to capture what my participants experienced in relation to the phenomenon, including specific examples given by individuals.

This process was in part facilitated and followed up by a more systematic approach to open coding, which delves deeper into the data to explore and harness all the content and nuances toward codes, subthemes, and themes.[15] Then I used axial coding, which extends the analysis that began with open coding, rearranging and reorganizing the data, refining and arriving at stable subthemes and themes.[16] I also bolstered my analysis by engaging with the multitude of documents that I gathered from the site visits, interviews, and participants. I embedded this information throughout the book, either when introducing individuals or weaving it throughout the stories of the educators as relevant. This integration provided a deeper level of context, complexity, and life to the participants, thus allowing me to better understand the humans that they are and the realities that they navigate.

A number of participants and cases inevitably received more coverage when presenting the findings. I did this intentionally for the sake of saliency and completeness of the themes and arguments, often best communicated when situated within a given participant's or case's holistic context. In addition, I did this due to the compelling nature and accessibility of the materials, but not at the cost of data saturation—meaning that the same themes and arguments came up over and over again without anything particularly new emerging as I continued to collect more interviews and information.[17] In cases where there were divergent findings, I recorded those instances in my own notes and made these complexities known throughout the book.

When developing this book, I also put the themes and subthemes from the interviews in conversation with the larger body of literature, policy, and practice in relation to community and technical colleges. This added contextual layer provides the broader scheme and basis on which

I further reconstructed my participants' experiences into narratives and stories interwoven throughout the book. This step allowed me to integrate my own critiques and reflections based on extant scholarship, policy, and practice. Because of the large number of interviews and stakeholder groups, I organized the book loosely but intentionally based on each salient group and the education topics engaged by the group. At the same time, the global sensemaking of the phenomenon captured in the book is at the meta-inference level, meaning that I used all the data from the project to develop a broader understanding through the integration of various sources.[18] The result of that meta-inference is the narratives, findings, and takeaways throughout the chapters, some of which are also presented as reflection questions at the end of chapters 1 through 8.

## HOW I ARRIVED AT TRUSTWORTHINESS

To ensure the findings that I present in this book are trustworthy, I performed several steps and strategies. First, in line with hermeneutic phenomenology and qualitative inquiry more broadly, I relied on reflexivity to confront my own position, assumptions, and biases that can play a role in the research process and interpretation of the data and findings.[19] I did this throughout the research process, whether it was through my recorded reflections after interviews, noting them during analysis, and explicitly sharing my positionality as detailed next.

Second, multiple researcher involvement allows investigator triangulation and different perspectives when examining various aspects of the research process.[20] Specifically, Kelly Wickersham and a few other team members (Amy Prevost, Xiwei Zhu, and Peiwen Zheng) provided an extra careful eye for the data selection, analysis, and interpretation. It was through several iterations with them, particularly processing conflicting interpretations of findings, that I arrived at the clarity, depth, and nuance that gave me confidence in the stories and cases I presented in the book.

Third, throughout the process, I've shared findings, excerpts, and draft chapters of this book with some of my participants, an approach known as member checks or respondent validation.[21] Although there is mixed opinion regarding member checks due to inherent variance in interpretations, I intentionally asked my participants not to interpret the emergent findings and themes themselves, but rather to fine-tune their own perspectives and experiences related to the phenomenon.[22] In doing so, I hoped to develop a fuller understanding and representation of what my participants shared with me.[23] Intriguingly, it was through this process that some of my participants voiced concerns that their critiques might reflect poorly on their institutions, or in some cases, backfire on the hard work they've put in over the years to bring efforts to fruition, which ultimately led me to the decision of masking states as mentioned earlier in this appendix. Granted, this approach loses some nuance in terms of varying state contexts, organizational structures, policies, and politics. But given the broad parallels and saturation across themes and topics that transcend institutional and geographical contexts, I believe this is a worthwhile tradeoff, as I must respond to the concerns and realities of the practitioners and colleges in which they may continue to work for a long time.

## WHO I AM AS PART OF THE STUDY

Closely related, as an education researcher who is perpetually on the journey of learning and unlearning, my gender, racial, social, and professional identities directly shaped how I positioned myself and engaged with all facets of this research. I identify as an Asian woman and an immigrant from a well-educated background, with a great deal of resources and privilege working at a highly regarded research institution. Also, two of my professional identities are particularly relevant to this research. First, I am a mid-career, university-based researcher with an agenda that centers community and technical colleges. Some participants read my prior research or had heard my name before the interviews. I also worked with a few of my interviewees through collaborative research endeavors. It is hard to assess how this part of my role affected the research, but the least I could do was to stay as transparent as possible throughout the research process, acknowledging both my knowledge and the more important fact that, while I do know a lot about this sector, I personally never attended or worked at a community or technical college, and it is the practitioners' most authentic input and realities that give weight and texture to this research.

Also essential to note, and this is perhaps what brought me even closer to the topic of this book and helped me forge a greater connection with my participants, are my identities as a teacher, mentor, advisor, and colleague in higher education who, over the past few years, grappled with massive mental health challenges while trying to deliver my own promise to render holistic support to my students and colleagues, all while mitigating inequities that my students, colleagues, or I personally encountered. These shared identities and experiences allowed a heightened level of awareness and sensitivity when interacting with these individuals.[24]

Often, soon into the interviews, I found it was through the connections on these levels that my participants clearly opened up more, giving rich, extended descriptions of their experiences navigating challenges and tensions at multiple levels. Although the student populations we serve are different, the pandemic struggles seem to have so much palpability that's broadly shared among educators. Without prior design, I sometimes briefly shared, in reciprocity, my own experiences with the pandemic, innovative solutions, and outstanding equity challenges, and on occasion, I exchanged tips and approaches that had worked (or not). Put simply, I found my participants connected with me at the salient core of this research—being an educator on a journey toward more equitably serving their students, striving for greater impact in sustainable ways.

I came into this work keenly aware of my various positionalities, assumptions, and biases, as well as tensions navigating my advocacy for and critiques of community and technical colleges. Although I will never know how my efforts transpired with 100 percent clarity or certainty, and that wasn't the goal, I did strive to be as transparent and responsive as possible to ensure that the interests and views of my participants were not neglected or marginalized. I hope that I have carried out and concluded this work in the spirit of responsibility, integrity, and humanity. More pressingly, I hope the reflective efforts covered by this book inspire innovative community and technical college research, policy, and practice that always drive—and are driven by—an unwavering commitment to achieving equity for students, educators, and these very institutions alike.

**TABLE A.1**  Background characteristics of all interviewed participants

| PARTICIPANT BACKGROUND | N | PERCENTAGE |
|---|---|---|
| *Gender identity* | | |
| Man | 56 | 44.4 |
| Woman | 67 | 53.2 |
| Nonbinary | 3 | 2.4 |
| *Racial/ethnic identity* | | |
| African American/Black | 12 | 9.7 |
| Asian | 10 | 8.1 |
| Latina/o/x | 11 | 8.9 |
| White | 81 | 65.3 |
| Multiracial | 8 | 6.5 |
| Indigenous | 2 | 1.6 |
| *Age* | | |
| 25–34 | 12 | 9.9 |
| 35–44 | 39 | 32.2 |
| 45–54 | 37 | 30.6 |
| 55–64 | 33 | 27.3 |
| *Social class* | | |
| Working class | 10 | 8.0 |
| Middle class | 61 | 48.8 |
| Upper-middle class | 52 | 41.6 |
| Wealthy | 2 | 1.6 |
| *Educational background* | | |
| Associate degree | 4 | 3.2 |
| Bachelor's degree | 24 | 19.0 |
| Master's degree | 42 | 33.3 |
| Doctorate or professional degree | 56 | 44.4 |
| *Role at the college* | | |
| Faculty | 48 | 38.1 |
| Staff | 26 | 20.6 |
| Administrator | 23 | 18.3 |
| Institutional researcher | 12 | 9.5 |
| Executive leader | 17 | 13.5 |

*Note.* Demographic characteristics are based on participant self-report. Role at the college is broadly categorized into five categories. Among faculty, seventeen were part time. Column counts within categories may not add up to 126, given that some participants did not provide full information. The "Percentage" column may not add up to 100 due to rounding.

**TABLE A.2** Interview participants featured in the book

| NAME | CHAPTERS THEY APPEARED IN | ROLE/POSITION | INSTITUTION (ALIAS) | REGION | RACIAL/ETHNIC IDENTITY | GENDER IDENTITY | AGE |
|---|---|---|---|---|---|---|---|
| Alberto | Intro, 1, 6 | President | West Bank College | Midwest | Latino | M | 45–54 |
| Alex | 6 | Dean, transportation | Nova Technical College | Midwest | White | M | 45–54 |
| Ali | 1, 3 | Vice president, learning | Midtown College | Midwest | Middle eastern | M | 55–64 |
| Anthony | 3, 5 | Executive director, student services | Parkfield Technical College | Midwest | White | M | 55–64 |
| Ashley | 2, 6 | Faculty member, psychology | Skyview Technical College | Midwest | White | W | 35–44 |
| Asia | 3 | Student support advisor | Keystone College | Midwest | Hmong (Asian) | M | 35–44 |
| Athena | 6 | Associate vice president, academic services | Lakefront College | Midwest | White | W | 45–54 |
| Behi | 2 | Faculty member, engineering technology | Ridgeline Technical College | Midwest | White (Persian) | M | 35–44 |
| Boricua | Intro, 1, 3, 4, 6 | Vice president, student services; assistant dean and registrar | Afton Community College | South | Latino | M | 45–54 |
| Brad [a] | 2, 6 | Faculty member, manufacturing | Prairie College | Midwest | White | M | 45–54 |
| Brayton | 6 | Faculty member and director, Center for Teaching and Learning | Keystone College | Midwest | Multiracial | M | 35–44 |
| Carl | 4, 8 | Dean of STEM | Inland Community College | West | African American/ Black | M | 45–54 |
| Casey | 1, 2, 6 | Director, Center for Teaching and Learning | Midtown College | Midwest | White | W | 45–54 |
| Chua | 3, 5 | Academic advisor and coordinator, community engagement | Keystone College | Midwest | Hmong (Asian) | W | 35–44 |
| Claudia | Intro, 1, 5, 6 | Coordinator, student services | Midwestern State Association of Colleges | Midwest | White | W | 25–34 |
| Clive | 5 | Specialist, organizational effectiveness | Midwestern State Association of Colleges | Midwest | White | M | 25–34 |
| Daniela | 1, 2 | Academic support specialist, Learning Center | Ridgeline Technical College | Midwest | Multiracial | W | 45–54 |

**TABLE A.2** *(continued)* Interview participants featured in the book

| NAME | CHAPTERS THEY APPEARED IN | ROLE/POSITION | INSTITUTION (ALIAS) | REGION | RACIAL/ETHNIC IDENTITY | GENDER IDENTITY | AGE |
|---|---|---|---|---|---|---|---|
| *Dave* | 2 | Faculty member, agriculture | Nova Technical College | Midwest | White | M | 35–44 |
| *David* | 1, 3, 5, 6 | Provost; faculty member and department chair | Central State College | South | African American/ Black | M | 45–54 |
| *Elizabeth* | 5 | Vice president, learning | Midwest Technical College | Midwest | White | W | 45–54 |
| *Esther* | 1, 2 | Faculty member, early childhood education | Lakefront College | Midwest | White | W | 35–44 |
| *Ethan* [a] | 5, 6 | Faculty member, biology | Oakwood Technical College | Midwest | White | M | 45–54 |
| *Eve* | 7 | Faculty member, biology | Midwest Technical College | Midwest | White | W | 25–34 |
| *Ginger* | 6 | Faculty member and department head, agriculture | Nova Technical College | Midwest | White | W | 45–54 |
| *Gretchen* | 7 | Associate dean, general education | Midwest Technical College | Midwest | White | W | 45–54 |
| *Helen* | 6, 8 | Vice president | Midwestern State Association of Colleges | Midwest | White | W | 55–64 |
| *Irene* | 3 | Associate dean, learner support and transition | Ridgeline Technical College | Midwest | White | W | 45–54 |
| *Janet* | 4 | Director, institutional research | Meadowland Technical College | Midwest | White | W | 45–54 |
| *Jeremy* [a] | 3 | Instructor and advisor, academic intervention | Ridgeline Technical College | Midwest | White | M | 25–34 |
| *Jill* | 4 | Enrollment management analyst; previously academic advisor | Keystone College | Midwest | White | W | 35–44 |
| *John* | Intro, 6 | Vice president, academic affairs | Pointe College | West | White | M | 55–64 |
| *Kayla* | 1, 6 | Faculty member, nursing; coach, Center for Teaching and Learning | Midtown College | Midwest | African American/ Black | W | 55–64 |

| Name | | Role | College | Region | Race/ethnicity | Gender | Age |
|---|---|---|---|---|---|---|---|
| *Kevin* | 3, 7 | Academic advisor | Midwest Technical College | Midwest | African American/ Black | M | 45–54 |
| *Lauren* | 4, 6 | Vice president, academic affairs | Keystone College | Midwest | White | W | 35–44 |
| *Linda* [a] | 6 | Faculty member, biology | Keystone College | Midwest | White | W | 55–64 |
| *Lindsey* [a] | 6 | Faculty member and program director, chemistry | Walt County College | West | White | W | 45–54 |
| *Lisa* [a] | 1, 2 | Faculty member, world languages | Keystone College | Midwest | White | W | 45–54 |
| *Liz* | 2, 4 | Faculty member, mathematics | Trailhead College | Midwest | White | W | 35–44 |
| *Maggie* | 5 | Faculty member, mathematics | Grassland College | South | White | W | 55–64 |
| *Marie* | 1, 6 | Faculty member, biology | Keystone College | Midwest | White | W | 45–54 |
| *Marques* | 6 | Dean, manufacturing, agriculture, and construction | Nova Technical College | Midwest | White | M | 55–64 |
| *Mary* | 7 | Faculty member, chemistry | Midwest Technical College | Midwest | White | W | 25–34 |
| *Mateo* | 1, 4 | Faculty member and program director, human services | Keystone College | Midwest | Latinx and Indigenous | M | 35–44 |
| *Maureen* | 4, 6 | Vice president, institutional effectiveness | Midtown College | Midwest | White | W | 45–54 |
| *Mavis* | 5 | Assistant director, admissions and transfer | Heartland Consortium | Midwest | White | W | 55–64 |
| *Michelle* | 2, 6 | Faculty member, chemistry | Coppice College | Midwest | White | W | 45–54 |
| *MJ* | 5 | Chief officer | Midwestern State Association of Colleges | Midwest | White | W | 55–64 |
| *Paddy* | 3 | Coordinator, reentry education services | Ridgeline Technical College | Midwest | White | M | 35–44 |
| *Peder* [a] | 2, 6 | Faculty member, graphic design | Glacier Technical College | Midwest | Asian | M | 55–64 |
| *Peter* | 7 | Faculty member, biology; associate dean, general education | Midwest Technical College | Midwest | White | M | 35–44 |
| *Polly* | 2 | Faculty member, nursing | Keystone College | Midwest | White | W | 55–64 |

**TABLE A.2** *(continued)* Interview participants featured in the book

| NAME | CHAPTERS THEY APPEARED IN | ROLE/POSITION | INSTITUTION (ALIAS) | REGION | RACIAL/ETHNIC IDENTITY | GENDER IDENTITY | AGE |
|---|---|---|---|---|---|---|---|
| *Precious* | 3, 6 | Dean, health sciences | Afton Community College | South | African American/ Black | W | 55–64 |
| *Reggie* | 3 | Dean, student access and success | Keystone College | Midwest | African American/ Black | M | 35–44 |
| *Renee* | Intro, 1, 5, 6 | Vice president, academic affairs and faculty development | Keystone College | Midwest | White | W | 55–64 |
| *Rosalia* | 5 | Assistant director, general education and transfer | Midwestern State Association of Colleges | Midwest | Latina | W | 35–44 |
| *Rose* | 7 | Faculty member, physics | Midwest Technical College | Midwest | White | W | 35–44 |
| *Rose R.* | 6 | Interim chief academic officer | Nova Technical College | Midwest | White | W | 35–44 |
| *Ruth* | 5 | President | Crosswind College | Midwest | White | W | 45–54 |
| *Samantha* | 5, 7 | Faculty member, chemistry | Midwest Technical College | Midwest | White | W | 35–44 |
| *Sharon* | 5 | Vice president, academic affairs | Parkfield Technical College | Midwest | White | W | 55–64 |
| *Shawn* | Intro, 2, 4 | Faculty member and department head, biology | Keystone College | Midwest | African American/ Black | M | 45–54 |
| *Sonya* | 3, 4 | Vice president, administration | Keystone College | Midwest | Latina | W | 35–44 |
| *Steph* | 8 | Administrative chair, general education | Parkfield Technical College | Midwest | White | W | 35–44 |
| *Steven* | 7 | Faculty member and program director, biology | Midwest Technical College | Midwest | White | M | 35–44 |
| *Sue* | 4, 6 | Director, institutional research | Midtown College | Midwest | Asian | W | 45–54 |
| *Todd* | 5 | Dean of STEM | West Grove College | Midwest | Asian | M | 55–64 |
| *Toni* | 6 | Faculty member and program director, industrial safety | Keystone College | Midwest | African American/ Black | W | 35–44 |

| | | | | | | | |
|---|---|---|---|---|---|---|---|
| TJ [a] | 5 | Faculty member, facilities management | Midtown College | Midwest | White | M | 55–64 |
| Veronica | 5 | Director, STEM programs; faculty member, mathematics | Gateway University | Midwest | White | W | 55–64 |
| Victoria | 4 | Director, institutional research | Keystone College | Midwest | Hmong (Asian) | W | 45–54 |
| Virginia | 1, 5, 6 | Faculty member, biotechnology | Keystone College | Midwest | White | W | 45–54 |
| Wade | 1, 6, 8 | President | Nova Technical College | Midwest | White | M | 45–54 |
| William | 2 | Faculty member, journalism | Keystone College | Midwest | White | M | 55–64 |

*Note.* STEM = science, technology, engineering, and mathematics.

1. Participants are listed alphabetically based on their pseudonyms. To ensure anonymity to the largest extent possible, all participants and institutions are given pseudonyms. Participants were invited to come up with their own study names, and the vast majority ended up doing so. The rest didn't have a preference, in which case I assigned them pseudonyms.

2. This table only lists background information of the participants featured in the book, although the themes and arguments made throughout the book are based on the interviews with all participants.

3. W = Woman, M = Man; no featured participants identified as gender nonbinary.

4. [a] denotes faculty with part-time experience or status.

5. For participants who described different positions held that are relevant to the interview questions, these positions are listed under the role/position column, separated with a ";" and starting with the most recent one.

# NOTES

PREFACE

1. Kelly Meyerhofer, "Plumbing, Nursing, Welding: How Are Hands-on MATC Programs Moving Online amid COVID-19 Pandemic?," *Wisconsin State Journal,* March 30, 2020, https://madison.com/news/local/education/university/ plumbing-nursing-welding-how-are-hands-on-matc-programs-moving-online- amid-covid-19-pandemic/article_a0c9942e-e0a6-5338-a149-3f2a43b6dff0.html.

2. League for Innovation in the Community College, *The Nature of Innovation in the Community College* (Chandler, AZ: League for Innovation in the Community College, 2010), https://www.league.org/sites/default/files/private_data/imported/ league_books/Nature%20of%20Innovation%20Report_FINAL.pdf; Terry O'Banion, Laura Weidner, and Cynthia Wilson, "Creating a Culture of Innovation in the Community College," *Community College Journal of Research and Practice* 35, no. 6 (2011): 470–483, https://doi.org/10.1080/10668926.2010.515508; Terry O'Banion, Laura Weidner, and Cynthia Wilson, "The Impact of Innovation," *Community College Journal of Research and Practice* 36, no. 1 (2012): 4–14, https:// doi.org/10.1080/10668926.2011.567161.

3. Jolanta Juszkiewicz, *Trends in Community College Enrollment and Completion Data, Issue 6* (Washington, DC: American Association of Community Colleges, 2020), https://www.aacc.nche.edu/wp-content/uploads/2020/08/Final_CC-Enrollment- 2020_730_1.pdf.

4. Mary Ellen Flannery, "Community College Faculty Fear COVID-19 Will Deepen Inequities," *neaToday,* April 16, 2020, https://www.nea.org/nea-today/all-news- articles/community-college-faculty-fear-covid-19-will-deepen-inequities.

5. I was fortunate to receive a grant from the National Science Foundation (NSF; award number DUE-2100029) for this research. With this support from the NSF, and also supplementary funds provided by the endowed chair that I hold owing to the generous support of the Barbara and Glenn Thompson family, I was able to devote time and resources to conducting a considerably large number of qualitative interviews and site visits that undergird the research presented in this book.

# INTRODUCTION

1. For participants featured multiple times in the book, at their first reference, I provide the pseudonyms of their institutions, often along with the larger geographical regions where the institutions are located. This information is not always repeated for subsequent appearances of the same participants unless it is integral to the experiences or ideas being presented. Table A.2 in the methodological appendix provides additional information about each of the featured participants. For details regarding the anonymity and protection of participants' identities, see the methodological appendix.

2. Matthew Zeidenberg, Davis Jenkins, and Marc A. Scott, *Not Just Math and English: Courses That Pose Obstacles to Community College Completion* (CCRC Working Paper No. 52), Community College Research Center (New York: Teachers College, Columbia University, 2012), https://ccrc.tc.columbia.edu/media/k2/attachments/not-just-math-and-english.pdf.

3. Arthur M. Cohen, Florence B. Brawer, and Carrie B. Kisker, *The American Community College* (San Francisco: Jossey-Bass, 2014).

4. Cohen, Brawer, and Kisker, *The American Community College.*

5. Nancy Shulock, Colleen Moore, and Jeremy Offenstein, *The Road Less Traveled: Realizing the Potential of Career Technical Education in the California Community Colleges* (Sacramento, CA: Institute for Higher Education Leadership & Policy, 2011), https://edinsightscenter.org/Portals/0/ReportPDFs/road-less-traveled.pdf?ver=2016-01-15-155407-347.

6. To be fair, these technical definitions are more reminiscent of various social, historical, economic, and political circumstances and intricacies than offering clarity to the already messy topic; my discussion on the terms is meant to provide a glimpse into the innumerable responsibilities, pressures, tensions, and yet possibilities that reside within these institutions.

7. Bill Hussar et al., *The Condition of Education 2020* (Washington, DC: US Department of Education, 2020), https://nces.ed.gov/pubs2020/2020144.pdf.

8. Thomas Brock and Cameron Diwa, "Catastrophe or Catalyst? Reflections on COVID's Impact on Community Colleges," *Journal of Postsecondary Student Success* 1, no. 2 (2021): 2–17, https://doi.org/10.33009/fsop_jpss129901.

9. Carol Cutler White, "The College Completion Agenda: Managing and Leading Change," *New Directions for Community Colleges* 2022, no. 198 (2022): 171–183, https://doi.org/10.1002/cc.20519; Achieving the Dream, *Community Colleges as Hubs of Social and Equitable Mobility and Equitable, Antiracist Communities: Achieving the Dream's Strategic Vision 2021–2025*, https://achievingthedream.org/wp-content/uploads/2022/07/ATD_2022_StratPlan-V4.pdf.

10. Universities of Wisconsin, "UW System Restructuring Is Given Seal of Approval by the Higher Learning Commission," https://www.wisconsin.edu/news/archive/uw-system-restructuring-is-given-seal-of-approval-by-the-higher-learning-commission/.

11. Board of Regents of the University System of Georgia, *Recommended Consolidations*, https://www.usg.edu/assets/usg/docs/consolidations.pdf; Doug Lederman, "From 3 Struggling Public Colleges, a New University Emerges," *Inside Higher Ed*, August 24, 2022, https://www.insidehighered.com/news/2022/08/24/3-struggling-public-colleges-new-university-emerges.

12. National Center for Education Statistics, "Digest of Education Statistics," US Department of Education, https://nces.ed.gov/programs/digest/.

13. Hilary Barker et al., *Early Impacts of COVID-19 Pandemic on the Wisconsin Technical College System* (Madison: Wisconsin Technical College System, 2021), https://www.wtcsystem.edu/assets/Covid-Spring-2020-Research-Brief.pdf; Brock and Diwa, "Catastrophe or Catalyst?"; National Student Clearinghouse Research Center, "Fall 2022 Stay Informed Report (09.29)," https://public.tableau.com/app/profile/researchcenter/viz/Fall2022StayInformedReport09_29/StayInformedFall2022.

14. Jennifer Causey et al., *COVID-19 Transfer, Mobility, and Progress*, Report No. 2, National Student Clearinghouse Research Center (Herndon, VA: National Student Clearinghouse Research Center, 2020), https://nscresearchcenter.org/wp-content/uploads/Covid19-TransferMobilityProgress-FinalFall2020.pdf.

15. Jennifer Causey et al., *Completing College: National and State Report with Longitudinal Data Dashboard on Six- and Eight-Year Completion Rates* (Signature Report 21), National Student Clearinghouse Research Center (Herndon, VA: National Student Clearinghouse Research Center, 2022), https://nscresearchcenter.org/wp-content/uploads/Completions_Report_2022.pdf.

16. Achieving the Dream, "Our Work," https://achievingthedream.org/our-work/. Achieving the Dream is a network that partners with colleges to support evidence-based change toward student success. Community College Research Center, "Guided Pathways," Columbia University, https://ccrc.tc.columbia.edu/research/guided-pathways.html. Guided Pathways is an empirically based reform model targeted at redesigning entire college programs and supports for smoother, successful college pathways for students. League for Innovation in the Community College, "About," https://www.league.org/about. The League for Innovation in the Community College is an organization that supports community and technical colleges in facilitating innovation and student success. Elizabeth Cox Brand, ed., *Student Success Center Network* (Hoboken, NJ: Wiley, 2023). The Student Success Center Network is a national network that aims to help colleges address equity issues toward improving student attainment of postsecondary qualifications.

17. Thomas R. Bailey, Shanna Smith Jaggars, and Davis Jenkins, *Redesigning America's Community Colleges: A Clearer Path to Student Success* (Cambridge, MA: Harvard University Press, 2015); Constance M. Carroll and Rufus Glasper, eds., *The Community College Baccalaureate: Supporting Regional Economic Development* (Chandler, AZ: League for Innovation in the Community College, 2018), https://foothill.edu/news/The%20Community%20College%20Baccalaureate_Supporting%20Regional%20Economic%20Development.pdf; Deborah L. Floyd,

"Achieving the Baccalaureate Through the Community College," *New Directions for Community Colleges* 2006, no. 135 (2006): 59–72, https://doi.org/10.1002/cc.248; Valerie Crespín-Trujillo and Matthew T. Hora, "Teaching During a Pandemic: Insights into Faculty Teaching Practices and Implications for Future Improvement," *New Directions for Community Colleges* 2021, no. 195 (2021): 13–22, https://doi.org/10.1002/cc.20463.

18. Anjalé D. Welton and Eboni M. Zamani-Gallaher, "Introduction and Overview of the Yearbook: Facilitating Institutional Change for Racial Equity in the Educational Pipeline," *Teachers College Record* 120, no. 14 (2018): 1–8, https://doi.org/10.1177/016146811812001408.

19. These are broad categories that capture the diversity of the roles of the institutional members in my study. My sample includes diverse and finer roles within each of these broad categories (e.g., part-time faculty, institutional researchers, advisors, deans, and presidents), which I present in the appending tables and describe in detail when introducing interview participants in the book.

20. John S. Levin, "Understandings of Community Colleges in Need of Resuscitation: The Case of Community College Faculty," in *Understanding Community Colleges*, ed. John S. Levin and Susan T. Kater (New York: Routledge, 2013), 233–254.

## CHAPTER 1

1. We analyzed the news stories and other website items embedded as hyperlinks in the weekly newsletters published by the state system office. We set the search window to March 2020 to May 2021, and curated fifty-nine newsletters in which 1,215 unique, publicly accessible, web-based publications were embedded. We extracted these unique publications using Python and imported these items into R. To help harness the large volume of text data that we extracted with research-informed judgment, we applied text mining techniques facilitated by qualitative coding. First, through an interactive process of reading the titles of the 1,215 publications, we identified thirty-nine broad categories of institutional responses and adaptations. This qualitative, manual process helped reveal the types of change and innovations that have occurred. Then, we used these thirty-nine categories to harness the data further using the pattern matching function in R. This procedure allowed us to identify the presence or absence of activities, efforts, and initiatives falling under one or more of the categories through matching keywords in the web items with the identified categories. We also presented these responses and adaptations against the time frame of our search, which allowed us to see how they evolved over time.

2. William A. Smith, "Black Faculty Coping with Racial Battle Fatigue: The Campus Racial Climate in a Post–Civil Rights Era," in *A Long Way to Go: Conversations About Race by African American Faculty and Graduate Students*, ed. Darrell Cleveland (New York: Peter Lang, 2004), 171–190.

3. Amy E. Brown and Susan Bickerstaff, "Committing to Instructional Improvement in an Era of Community College Reform," *New Directions for Community Colleges* 2021, no. 195 (2021): 129–142, http://doi.org/10.1002/cc.20472; Catherine L. Finnegan, "The Multiple Roles of Faculty in Supporting Community College Students," *New Directions for Community Colleges* 2019, no. 187 (2019): 63–72, http://doi.org/10.1002/cc.20370; Xiaodan Hu, "Building an Equalized Technology-Mediated Advising Structure: Academic Advising at Community Colleges in the Post-COVID-19 Era," *Community College Journal of Research and Practice* 44, no. 10–12 (2020): 914–920, http://doi.org/10.1080/10668926.2020.1798304; Two-Year College English Association, *White Paper on Two-Year College English Faculty Workload* (Champaign, IL: National Council of Teachers of English, 2021), https://ncte.org/wp-content/uploads/2021/04/TYC_English_Faculty_Workload.pdf.

## CHAPTER 2

1. Regina Deil-Amen, "Socio-Academic Integrative Moments: Rethinking Academic and Social Integration Among Two-Year College Students in Career-Related Programs," *Journal of Higher Education* 82, no. 1 (2011): 54–91; Lauren Schudde, "Short- and Long-Term Impacts of Engagement Experiences with Faculty and Peers at Community Colleges," *Review of Higher Education* 42, no. 2 (2019): 385–426, https://doi.org/10.1353/rhe.2019.0001; Xueli Wang, *On My Own: The Challenge and Promise of Building Equitable STEM Transfer Pathways* (Cambridge, MA: Harvard Education Press, 2020).

2. Robert K. Frank, "Don't Kid Yourself: Online Lectures Are Here to Stay," *New York Times*, June 5, 2020, https://www.nytimes.com/2020/06/05/business/online-learning-winner-coronavirus.html; Avriel Epps-Darling, "Virtual Learning Might Be the Best Thing to Happen to Schools," *The Atlantic*, March 17, 2021, https://www.theatlantic.com/culture/archive/2021/03/virtual-learning-could-make-person-school-better/618297/.

3. Thomas R. Bailey, Shanna Smith Jaggars, and Davis Jenkins, *Redesigning America's Community Colleges: A Clearer Path to Student Success* (Cambridge, MA: Harvard University Press, 2015).

4. Bailey, Jaggars, and Jenkins, *Redesigning America's Community Colleges*.

5. Tressie McMillan-Cottom and Celeste Watkins-Hayes, "Dr. Tressie McMillan-Cottom on Modern Discourse" (speaker series, University of Michigan, Ann Arbor, March 17, 2021).

6. Cornell University, "Universal Design for Learning," https://teaching.cornell.edu/teaching-resources/designing-your-course/universal-design-learning.

7. Cassandra M.D. Hart et al., "COVID-19 and Community College Instructional Responses," *Online Learning Journal* 25, no. 1 (2021): 41–69, https://files.eric.ed.gov/fulltext/EJ1287109.pdf.

8. Claire H. Major, *Teaching Online: A Guide to Theory, Research, and Practice* (Baltimore, MD: Johns Hopkins University Press, 2015); Kathryn Linder and

Chrysanthemum Mattison Hayes, eds., *High-Impact Practices in Online Education: Research and Best Practices* (Sterling, VA: Stylus, 2018); Stephanie J. Blackmon, "Teaching Online, Challenges and Motivations: A Research Synthesis," *Education Matters: Journal of Teaching and Learning* 4, no. 1 (2016): 66–83; Stephanie J. Blackmon and Claire Major, "Student Experiences in Online Courses: A Qualitative Research Synthesis," *Quarterly Review of Distance Education* 13, no. 2 (2012): 77–85; Katrina A. Meyer, "Quality in Distance Education: Focus on On-line Learning," in *ASHE-ERIC Higher Education Report*, ed. Adrianna J. Kezar (Hoboken, NJ: Wiley, 2002): 1–134.

9. Di Xu, Qiujie Li, and Xuehan Zhou, *Online Course Quality Rubric: A Tool Box* (Irvine, CA: Online Learning Research Center, 2020), https://www.olrc.us/uploads/1/2/7/1/127107452/rubric_full_version_0414.pdf.

10. Nancy Diekelmann, "Narrative Pedagogy: Heideggerian Hermeneutical Analyses of Lived Experiences of Students, Teachers, and Clinicians," *Advances in Nursing Science* 23, no. 3 (2001): 53–71.

11. Gloria Ladson-Billings, "Toward a Theory of Culturally Relevant Pedagogy," *American Educational Research Journal* 32, no. 3 (1995): 465–491, https://doi.org/10.3102/00028312032003465; Django Paris and H. Samy Alim, eds., *Culturally Sustaining Pedagogies: Teaching and Learning for Justice in a Changing World* (New York: Teachers College Press, 2017); Tara J. Yosso, "Whose Culture Has Capital? A Critical Race Theory Discussion of Community Cultural Wealth," *Race Ethnicity and Education* 8, no. 1 (2005): 69–91, https://doi.org/10.1080/1361332052000341006; Luis C. Moll and Norma González, "Lessons from Research with Language-Minority Children," *Journal of Reading Behavior* 26, no. 4 (1994): 439–456; Laura I. Rendón, "Validating Culturally Diverse Students: Toward a New Model of Learning and Student Development," *Innovative Higher Education* 19, no. 1 (1994): 33–51, https://doi.org/10.1007/BF01191156.

12. Arthur M. Cohen, Florence B. Brawer, and Carrie B. Kisker, *The American Community College* (San Francisco: Jossey-Bass, 2014).

13. Samantha L. Anders, Patricia A. Frazier, and Sandra L. Shallcross, "Prevalence and Effects of Life Event Exposure Among Undergraduate and Community College Students," *Journal of Counseling Psychology* 59, no. 3 (2012): 449–457, https://doi.org/10.1037/a0027753.

14. Daniela's work explored how trauma-informed academic supports could help formerly incarcerated individuals transition to a college environment, as well as ways to further improve these supports to enhance student success.

15. Centers for Disease Control and Prevention, *6 Guiding Principles to a Trauma-Informed Approach*, https://www.cdc.gov/orr/infographics/00_docs/TRAINING_EMERGENCY_RESPONDERS_FINAL_2022.pdf; Trauma-Informed Care Implementation Resource Center, *What Is Trauma-Informed Care?*, https://www.traumainformedcare.chcs.org/wp-content/uploads/Fact-Sheet-What-is-Trauma-Informed-Care.pdf.

16. Maria S. Cormier and Susan Bickerstaff, *How Can We Improve Teaching in Higher Education? Learning from CUNY Start* (CCRC Working Paper No. 120), Community College Research Center (New York: Teachers College, Columbia University, 2020), https://ccrc.tc.columbia.edu/media/k2/attachments/improving-teaching-cuny-start.pdf; Allison Kadlec, "Learning with Colleges About How to Enact Whole-College Reforms," *Mixed Methods Blog*, November 12, 2019, https://ccrc.tc.columbia.edu/easyblog/learning-colleges-enact-reforms.html.

17. "Decolonization" is a broader term that describes the process of interrogating and undoing colonial powers, structures, and practices ingrained in areas like history, society, culture, politics, the economy, education, and others that have enacted sovereignty and inflicted harm and trauma on Indigenous and other marginalized populations. In education, decolonization involves a process of reflecting on and confronting the power and oppression embedded in teaching, learning, and curricula that reaffirm whiteness and perpetuate inequities across student groups. In doing so, educators engage in intentional efforts to address these dynamics and structures, ranging from integrating, validating, and recentering diverse perspectives, cultures, and values to revising policies and practices that prioritize white norms and expectations that lead to inequitable outcomes, to cite just a couple of examples. See Edward C. Bush et al., "Liberatory Community College Leadership: Education, Decolonization, and Emancipation," *New Directions for Community Colleges* 2023, no. 202 (2023): 199–208, https://doi.org/10.1002/cc.20579; Santiago Andrés Garcia, "Contesting Trauma and Violence Through Indigeneity and a Decolonizing Pedagogy at Rio Hondo Community College," *Journal of Latinos and Education* 20, no. 4 (2021): 376–396, https://doi.org/10.1080/15348431.2019.1603749; Silvia Toscano Villanueva, "Teaching as a Healing Craft: Decolonizing the Classroom and Creating Spaces of Hopeful Resistance Through Chicano-Indigenous Pedagogical Praxis," *Urban Review* 45 (2013): 23–40, https://doi.org/10.1007/s11256-012-0222-5.

18. John S. Levin et al., "Community College Culture and Faculty of Color," *Community College Review* 42, no. 1 (2014): 55–74, https://doi.org/10.1177/0091552113512864; National Center for Education Statistics, "Characteristics of Postsecondary Faculty," US Department of Education, https://nces.ed.gov/programs/coe/indicator/csc/postsecondary-faculty.

## CHAPTER 3

1. Thomas R. Bailey, Shanna S. Jaggars, and Davis Jenkins, *Redesigning America's Community Colleges: A Clearer Path to Student Success* (Cambridge, MA: Harvard University Press, 2015); Xueli Wang, *On My Own: The Challenge and Promise of Building Equitable STEM Transfer Pathways* (Cambridge, MA: Harvard Education Press, 2020).

2. Clive Belfield and Thomas Brock, "Behind the Enrollment Numbers: How COVID Has Changed Students' Plans for Community College," *Mixed*

*Methods Blog*, November 19, 2020, https://ccrc.tc.columbia.edu/easyblog/covid-enrollment-community-college-plans.html; George Bulman and Robert Fairlie, "The Impact of COVID-19 on Community College Enrollment and Student Success: Evidence from California Administrative Data," *Education Finance and Policy* 17, no. 4 (2022): 745–764, https://doi.org/10.1162/edfp_a_00384.

3. Wang, *On My Own.*

4. US Department of Education, "CARES Act: Higher Education Emergency Relief Fund," https://www2.ed.gov/about/offices/list/ope/caresact.html.

5. Stephen J. Handel, "Aid and Advocacy: Why Community College Transfer Students Do Not Apply for Financial Aid and How Counselors Can Help Them Get in the Game," *Journal of College Admission* 201 (2008): 8–16.

6. Handel, "Aid and Advocacy"; Julia I. Lopez, "Unmet Need and Unclaimed Aid: Increasing Access to Financial Aid for Community College Students," *New Directions for Community Colleges* 2013, no. 164 (2013): 67–74, https://doi.org/10.1002/cc.20082; Lyle McKinney and Toya Roberts, "The Role of Community College Financial Aid Counselors in Helping Students Understand and Utilize Financial Aid," *Community College Journal of Research and Practice* 36, no. 10 (2012): 761–774, https://doi.org/10.1080/10668926.2011.585112.

7. Lijing Yang and Shannon Venezia, "The Impact of Financial Aid on Associate Degree Attainment for Rural Community College Students: A Comparison of Rural, Urban, and Suburban Patterns," *Community College Review* 48, no. 4 (2020): 423–454, https://doi.org/10.1177/0091552120935975; McKinney and Roberts, "Community College Financial Aid Counselors."

8. "Justice-involved" is a term used to humanize individuals who have interacted with the criminal justice system, focusing on their broader identity beyond their past actions.

9. Susan Bickerstaff et al., *Implementing and Scaling Multiple Measures Assessment in the Context of COVID-19* (Research Brief), Center for the Analysis of Postsecondary Readiness (New York: Teachers College, Columbia University, 2021), https://postsecondaryreadiness.org/wp-content/uploads/2021/01/multiple-measures-expansion-covid19.pdf; Katherine L. Hughes and Judith Scott-Clayton, "Assessing Developmental Assessment in Community Colleges," *Community College Review* 39, no. 4 (2011): 327–351, https://doi.org/10.1177/0091552111426898; Mary E. Kingan and Richard L. Alfred, "Entry Assessment in Community Colleges: Tracking or Facilitating?," *Community College Review* 21, no. 3 (1993): 3–16, https://doi.org/10.1177/009155219302100302.

10. Bailey, Jaggars, and Jenkins, *Redesigning America's Community Colleges.*

## CHAPTER 4

1. Tia B. McNair, Estela M. Bensimon, and Lindsey Malcom-Piqueux, *From Equity Talk to Equity Walk: Expanding Practitioner Knowledge for Racial Justice in Higher Education* (Hoboken, NJ: Wiley, 2020).

2. Keystone College's efforts to support students are based on the findings using text mining techniques and qualitative coding of news media, as detailed in chapter 1.

3. Cassandra M.D. Hart, Elizabeth Friedmann, and Michael Hill, "Online Course-Taking and Student Outcomes in California Community Colleges," *Education Finance and Policy* 13, no. 1 (2018): 42–71, https://doi.org/10.1162/edfp_a_00218.

4. Joshua Goodman, Julia Melkers, and Amanda Pallais, "Can Online Delivery Increase Access to Education?," *Journal of Labor Economics* 37, no. 1 (2019): 1–34; Shanna Smith Jaggars, *Online Learning: Does It Help Low-Income and Underprepared Students?* (CCRC Working Paper No. 26), Community College Research Center (New York: Teachers College, Columbia University, 2011), https://ccrc.tc.columbia.edu/media/k2/attachments/online-learning-help-students.pdf; Cameron Sublett, *Distant Equity: The Promise and Pitfalls of Online Learning for Students of Color in Higher Education* (Washington, DC: American Council on Education, 2020), http://www.equityinhighered.org/wp-content/uploads/2020/11/C.-Sublett-Essay-final.pdf; Di Xu and Ying Xu, *The Promises and Limits of Online Higher Education: Understanding How Distance Education Affects Access, Cost, and Quality* (Washington, DC: American Enterprise Institute, 2019), https://www.aei.org/wp-content/uploads/2019/03/The-Promises-and-Limits-of-Online-Higher-Education.pdf?x91208.

5. Elvira Abrica, "How to Measure Student Success? Toward Consideration of Student Resilience as a Metric of Success in Institutional Accountability Frameworks," *Community College Journal of Research and Practice* 42, no. 7–8 (2018): 569–573, https://doi.org/10.1080/10668926.2018.1429962; Thomas Bailey, D. Timothy Leinbach, and Davis Jenkins, *Is Student Success Labeled Institutional Failure? Student Goals and Graduation Rates in the Accountability Debate at Community Colleges* (CCRC Working Paper No. 1), Community College Research Center (New York: Teachers College, Columbia University, 2006), https://ccrc.tc.columbia.edu/media/k2/attachments/student-success-goals-graduation-rates.pdf; Michelle Dimino, *How Outcomes Metrics Can Better Reflect Community College Performance,* http://thirdway.imgix.net/pdfs/how-outcomes-metrics-can-better-reflect-community-college-performance.pdf; Kevin J. Dougherty et al., *Performance Accountability Systems for Community Colleges: Lessons for the Voluntary Framework of Accountability,* Community College Research Center (New York: Teachers College, Columbia University, 2009), https://ccrc.tc.columbia.edu/media/k2/attachments/performance-accountability-systems.pdf; Mia Ocean, Jeffrey McLaughlin, and Jacqueline Hodes, "'We Take EVERYONE': Perceptions of External Assessment and Accountability at the Community College," *Community College Journal of Research and Practice* 46, no. 4 (2022): 223–239, https://doi.org/10.1080/10668926.2020.1841041.

## CHAPTER 5

1. Gloria Crisp et al., "Empirical and Practical Implications for Documenting Early Racial Transfer Gaps," *New Directions for Community Colleges* 2020, no. 192 (2020):

55–65, https://doi.org/10.1002/cc.20423; Yuxin Lin, Maggie P. Fay, and John Fink, "Stratified Trajectories: Charting Equity Gaps in Program Pathways Among Community College Students," *Research in Higher Education* 64 (2023): 547–573, https://doi.org/10.1007/s11162-022-09714-7; Gelsey Mehl et al., *The Dual Enrollment Playbook: A Guide to Equitable Acceleration for Students* (Washington, DC: Aspen Institute, 2020), https://ccrc.tc.columbia.edu/media/k2/attachments/dual-enrollment-playbook-equitable-acceleration.pdf; Carrie Petrucci and Armando Rivera-Figueroa, "STEM Faculty Mentoring and Advising at an Urban Hispanic-Serving Community College," *Community College Journal of Research and Practice* (2022): 1–19, https://doi.org/10.1080/10668926.2022.2056549; Xueli Wang, *On My Own: The Challenge and Promise of Building Equitable STEM Transfer Pathways* (Cambridge, MA: Harvard Education Press, 2020); Carol C. White, "Advocating for Community Colleges in the College Completion Agenda," *New Directions for Community Colleges* 2022, no. 197 (2022): 157–173, https://doi.org/10.1002/cc.20504.

2. The college efforts described are based on the findings using text mining techniques and qualitative coding of news media as detailed in chapter 1.

3. North Carolina Community College System, "Community Colleges Donate Medical Supplies, Install Community WiFi, Help Small Businesses Survive COVID-19 Pandemic," *NC Community Colleges*, April 2, 2020, https://www.lsteam.org/newscenter/news/community-colleges-donate-medical-supplies-install-community-wifi-help-small; Pennsylvania Commission for Community Colleges, "More than 10 Community Colleges Donate Critical Supplies During Shortage Caused by COVID-19," April 3, 2020, https://pacommunitycolleges.org/2020/04/more-than-10-community-colleges-donate-critical-supplies-during-shortage-caused-by-covid-19/.

4. Mia Ocean, Lisa Calvano, and Marian McGorry, "Bridging the Gap Between the Community and the Ivory Tower: A Case Study of University–Community College Partnership Models," in *University–Community Partnerships for Promoting Social Responsibility in Higher Education,* ed. Enakshi Sengupta, Patrick Blessinger, and Craig Mahoney (Bingley, UK: Emerald, 2020), 201–213; Lauren Schudde, Huriya Jabbar, and Catherine Hartman, "How Political and Ecological Contexts Shape Community College Transfer," *Sociology of Education* 94, no. 1 (2021): 65–83, https://doi.org/10.1177/0038040720954817.

5. Wang, *On My Own.*

6. Pamela Brown et al., "Building Capacity: Enhancing Undergraduate STEM Education by Improving Transfer Success" (paper presented at the American Society for Engineering Education 2022 Annual Conference, Minneapolis, MN, June 26, 2022), 1–14; Alicia C. Dowd, "Developing Supportive STEM Community College to Four-Year College and University Transfer Ecosystems," in *Community Colleges in the Evolving STEM Education Landscape: Summary of a Summit* (Washington, DC: National Academies Press, 2012), 107–134; Raquel Harper and

Heather Thiry, "Advising from Community College to University: What It Takes for Underrepresented Transfer Students in STEM to Succeed," *Community College Journal of Research and Practice* (2022): 1–20, https://doi.org/10.1080/106689 26.2022.2050842; Bethany Sansing-Helton, Gail Coover, and Charles E. Benton Jr., "Increasing STEM Transfer Readiness Among Underrepresented Minoritized Two-Year College Students: Examining Course-Taking Patterns, Experiences, and Interventions," *Frontiers in Education* 6 (2021): 1–17, https://doi.org/10.3389/feduc.2021.667091; Wang, *On My Own*.

7. Elisabeth Barnett and Liesa Stamm, *Dual Enrollment: A Strategy for Educational Advancement of All Students* (Washington, DC: Blackboard Institute, 2010); Jason L. Taylor, "Accelerating Pathways to College: The (In)Equitable Effects of Community College Dual Credit," *Community College Review* 43, no. 4 (2015): 355–379, https://doi.org/10.1177/0091552115594880.

## CHAPTER 6

1. Kevin McClure, "Burnout Is Coming to Campus: Are College Leaders Ready?," *EdSurge*, August 14, 2020, https://www.edsurge.com/news/2020-08-14-burnout-is-coming-to-campus-are-college-leaders-ready; Kevin McClure, "Don't Blame the Pandemic for Worker Discontent," *Chronicle of Higher Education*, May 27, 2022, https://www.chronicle.com/article/dont-blame-the-pandemic-for-worker-discontent; Kevin McClure, "Higher Ed, We've Got a Morale Problem—And a Free T-Shirt Won't Fix It," *EdSurge*, September 27, 2021, https://www.edsurge.com/news/2021-09-27-higher-ed-we-ve-got-a-morale-problem-and-a-free-t-shirt-won-t-fix-it; Kevin McClure and Alisa Hicklin Fryar, "The Great Faculty Disengagement," *Chronicle of Higher Education*, January 19, 2022, https://www.chronicle.com/article/the-great-faculty-disengagement; Doug Lederman, "Turnover, Burnout and Demoralization in Higher Ed," *Inside Higher Ed*, May 3, 2022, https://www.insidehighered.com/news/2022/05/04/turnover-burnout-and-demoralization-higher-ed; Kevin McClure et al., *The Impact of COVID-19 on Faculty, Staff, and Students: Using Research to Help Higher Education Heal Through the Pandemic and Beyond*, https://www.ashe.ws/Files/Position%20Taking/2023.01%20ASHE%20Statement%20on%20The%20Impact%20of%20COVID-19.pdf.

2. Leslie D. Gonzales and David F. Ayers, "The Convergence of Institutional Logics on the Community College Sector and the Normalization of Emotional Labor: A New Theoretical Approach for Considering the Community College Faculty Labor Expectations," *Review of Higher Education* 41, no. 3 (2018): 455–478, https://doi.org/10.1353/rhe.2018.0015.

3. Marilyn J. Amey, "Beyond the Competencies: Adaptive Community College Leadership," in *Higher Education: Handbook of Theory and Research*, ed. Laura W. Perna (Cham, Switzerland: Springer, 2022), 417–435; Marilyn J. Amey and Pamela L. Eddy, "Leading in the Middle," in *Understanding Community Colleges*,

ed. John S. Levin and Susan T. Kater (New York: Routledge, 2018), 203–225; Pamela L. Eddy, *Community College Leadership: A Multidimensional Model for Leading Change* (Sterling, VA: Stylus, 2010).

4. Cheryl J. Daly, "Faculty Learning Communities: Addressing the Professional Development Needs of Faculty and the Learning Needs of Students," *Currents in Teaching & Learning* 4, no. 1 (2011): 3–16; Pamela L. Eddy et al., "Fostering Communities of Practice Among Community College Science Faculty," *Community College Review* 50, no. 4 (2022): 391–414, https://doi.org/10.1177/00915521221111474.

5. Florence B. Brawer, "Faculty Development: The Literature," *Community College Review* 18, no. 1 (1990): 50–56; Daly, "Faculty Learning Communities"; John P. Murray, "The Current State of Faculty Development in Two-Year Colleges," *New Directions for Community Colleges* 2002, no. 118 (2002): 89–98, https://doi.org/10.1002/cc.67.

## CHAPTER 7

1. Xueli Wang, *On My Own: The Challenge and Promise of Building Equitable STEM Transfer Pathways* (Cambridge, MA: Harvard Education Press, 2020).

2. Achieving the Dream, *Preparing for Shortened Academic Terms: A Guide* (Silver Spring, MD: Achieving the Dream, 2022), https://achievingthedream.org/wp-content/uploads/2022/05/atd_preparing_shortened_terms_guide.pdf; Davis Jenkins, Hana Lahr, and Amy Mazzariello, *How to Achieve More Equitable Community College Student Outcomes: Lessons from Six Years of CCRC Research on Guided Pathways* (New York: Community College Research Center, 2021), https://ccrc.tc.columbia.edu/media/k2/attachments/equitable-community-college-student-outcomes-guided-pathways.pdf; Hamnah Malik, "Moving Beyond Semester vs. Quarter System," *Mixed Methods Blog*, January 23, 2023, https://ccrc.tc.columbia.edu/easyblog/moving-beyond-semester-vs-quarter-system.html.

## CHAPTER 8

1. Maria Carrasco, "Fewer High School Graduates Go Straight to College," *Inside Higher Ed*, January 6, 2022, https://www.insidehighered.com/news/2022/01/07/fewer-high-school-graduates-enroll-college; Allan Golston, "Understanding Why a Growing Number of High School Graduates Are Choosing Not to Go to College… and What We Can Do About It," *Gates Foundation*, September 28, 2022, https://usprogram.gatesfoundation.org/news-and-insights/articles/understanding-why-a-growing-number-of-high-school-graduates-are-choosing-not-to-go-to-college; Davis Jenkins, "Why Has Community College Enrollment Declined and What Can We Do About It?," *Mixed Methods Blog*, May 1, 2023, https://ccrc.tc.columbia.edu/easyblog/why-enrollment-declined-what-can-we-do.html; Jon Marcus, "How Higher Education Lost Its Shine: Americans Are Rejecting College in Record Numbers, but the Reasons May Not Be What You Think," *Hechinger Report*, August 10, 2022, https://hechingerreport.org/

how-higher-education-lost-its-shine/; Katharine Meyer, "The Case for College: Promising Solutions to Reverse College Enrollment Declines," *Brown Center Chalkboard*, June 5, 2023, https://www.brookings.edu/blog/brown-center-chalkboard/2023/06/05/the-case-for-college-promising-solutions-to-reverse-college-enrollment-declines/.

2. "Achieving the Dream," https://achievingthedream.org. Achieving the Dream is a network founded in 2004 by the Lumina Foundation for Education, with its main goal being to improve community college student success. From the get-go, the network aspires to operate with a strong equity premise, bringing to the fore-front the academic progress and outcomes of low-income students and students of color. Another strong anchor is a culture of evidence that engages data to track student academic progress. This emphasis has contributed to expanded institutional research capacity at many community colleges.

3. Community College Research Center, "Guided Pathways," https://ccrc.tc.columbia.edu/research/guided-pathways.html. Guided Pathways is a movement acting highly in concert with Achieving the Dream. It started to gain widespread traction notably after Thomas R. Bailey, Shanna Smith Jaggars, and Davis Jenkins outlined the model in their book, *Redesigning America's Community Colleges: A Clearer Path to Student Success* (Cambridge, MA: Harvard University Press, 2015). Set out to achieve organizational level change, the Guided Pathways model aims to improve student outcomes by restructuring colleges' programs and student support in four broad areas: clear program paths, new student onboarding, academic support and advising, and teaching and learning. These efforts have evolved over the years, with the most recently integrated emphasis on equity.

4. Heather N. McCambly et al., "Community Colleges as Racialized Organizations: Outlining Opportunities for Equity," *Community College Review* (2023), https://doi.org/10.1177/00915521231182121.

5. Center for Urban Education, University of Southern California, "Developing a Practice of Equity Minded Indicators," https://bpb-us-e1.wpmucdn.com/sites.usc.edu/dist/6/735/files/2016/02/Developing-a-Practice-of-Equity-Mindedness.pdf.

6. Lorenzo DuBois Baber et al., "From Access to Equity: Community Colleges and the Social Justice Imperative," in *Higher Education: Handbook of Theory and Research*, ed. Michael B. Paulsen and Laura W. Perna (Cham, Switzerland: Springer, 2019), 203–240.

7. McCambly et al., "Community Colleges as Racialized Organizations."

8. Adrianna Kezar, *How Colleges Change* (New York: Routledge, 2018).

9. Deborah Loewenberg Ball, "(What) Does Practice-Based Teacher Education Have to Do with Disrupting Racism and Oppression?," https://static1.squarespace.com/static/577fc4e2440243084a67dc49/t/5b4f601c575d1feb288a4cac/1531928609258/071618_PBTE.pdf; KerryAnn O'Meara, "Leveraging,

Checking, and Structuring Faculty Discretion to Advance Full Participation," *Review of Higher Education* 44, no. 4 (2021): 555–585, https://www. advancepartnership.iastate.edu/files/inline-files/O%27Meara%20RHE%20 Leveraging%2C%20Checking%20and%20Structuring%20Faculty%20Discretion %20to%20Advance%20Full%20Participation.pdf.

10. Matthew T. Hora, *Beyond the Skills Gap: Preparing College Students for Life and Work* (Cambridge, MA: Harvard Education Press, 2019); Matthew T. Hora and Changhee Lee, "Does Industry Experience Increase the Teaching of 'Soft' Skills in Community College Classrooms?," *New Directions for Community Colleges* 2021, no. 195 (2021): 65–79, https://doi.org/10.1002/cc.20467. Hard skills refer to technical skills and competencies needed to perform roles and tasks in the workforce.

11. Joy Gaston Gayles, "Humanizing Higher Education: A Path Forward in Uncertain Times," *Review of Higher Education* 46, no. 4 (2023): 547–567, https://doi. org/10.1353/rhe.2023.a900572.

12. Hyflex is an instructional modality that consists of face-to-face, online livestream, and online asynchronous. Students can choose among these options when attending and participating in this type of modality.

## METHODOLOGICAL APPENDIX

1. A fully integrated mixed methods design involves a mixture of two strands, quantitative and qualitative, interactively across various stages of a study, at times concurrently and at others sequentially as needed. For example, in the larger project, the quantitative strand relied on text mining of documents and the qualitative adopted case studies using interview data. The text mining helped inform the case studies and participant selection for interviews, whereas findings from interviews and case studies helped refine the text mining process. A full integration of the strands occurred through meta-inference, or a broader explanation and understanding drawn from both strands of the study. Elizabeth G. Creamer, *An Introduction to Fully Integrated Mixed Methods Research* (Thousand Oaks, CA: SAGE, 2018); Charles Teddlie and Abbas Tashakkori, "A General Typology of Research Designs Featuring Mixed Methods," *Research in the Schools* 13, no. 1 (2006): 12–28; Charles Teddlie and Abbas Tashakkori, *Foundations of Mixed Methods Research: Integrating Quantitative and Qualitative Approaches in the Social and Behavioral Sciences* (Thousand Oaks, CA: SAGE, 2009).

2. Hans-Georg Gadamer, *Philosophical Hermeneutics* (Berkeley: University of California Press, 1976); Martin Heidegger, *Being and Time* (New York: Harper, 1962); Susann M. Laverty, "Hermeneutic Phenomenology and Phenomenology: A Comparison of Historical and Methodological Considerations," *International Journal of Qualitative Methods* 2, no. 3 (2003): 21–35.

3. Sharan B. Merriam and Elizabeth J. Tisdell, *Qualitative Research: A Guide to Design and Implementation* (San Francisco: Jossey-Bass, 2015); Heidegger, *Being and Time*; Gadamer, *Philosophical Hermeneutics*.

4. Heidegger, *Being and Time*; Max van Manen, *Researching Lived Experience: Human Science for an Action Sensitive Pedagogy* (New York: Routledge, 2016).

5. See van Manen, *Researching Lived Experience*.

6. Lesley Bartlett and Frances Vavrus, *Rethinking Case Study Research: A Comparative Approach* (New York: Routledge, 2017).

7. Michael Quinn Patton, *Qualitative Research & Evaluation Methods: Integrating Theory and Practice* (Thousand Oaks, CA: SAGE, 2015).

8. Matthew B. Miles and A. Michael Huberman, *Qualitative Data Analysis: An Expanded Sourcebook* (Thousand Oaks, CA: SAGE, 1994).

9. Heidegger, *Being and Time*; van Manen, *Researching Lived Experience*.

10. Laverty, "Hermeneutic Phenomenology"; van Manen, *Researching Lived Experience*.

11. Hans-Georg Gadamer, *Truth and Method* (New York: Continuum, 1998); Heidegger, *Being and Time*; van Manen, *Researching Lived Experience*.

12. Heidegger, *Being and Time*; Rosanna Hertz, *Reflexivity and Voice* (Thousand Oaks, CA: SAGE, 1997); Laverty, "Hermeneutic Phenomenology."

13. Nancy J. Moules et al., eds., *Conducting Hermeneutic Research: From Philosophy to Practice* (New York: Peter Lang, 2015).

14. Gadamer, *Truth and Method*.

15. Johnny Saldaña, *The Coding Manual for Qualitative Researchers* (Thousand Oaks, CA: SAGE, 2013).

16. Saldaña, *The Coding Manual for Qualitative Researchers*.

17. Merriam and Tisdell, *Qualitative Research*.

18. Abbas Tashakkori and Charles Teddlie, "Quality of Inferences in Mixed Methods Research: Calling for an Integrative Framework," *Advances in Mixed Methods Research* 53, no. 7 (2008): 101–119.

19. Gadamer, *Truth and Method*; Merriam and Tisdell, *Qualitative Research*.

20. Patton, *Qualitative Research & Evaluation Methods*.

21. Gadamer, *Truth and Method*; Laverty, "Hermeneutic Phenomenology"; Joseph A. Maxwell, *Qualitative Research Design: An Interactive Approach* (Thousand Oaks, CA: SAGE, 2012); Merriam and Tisdell, *Qualitative Research*.

22. Merriam and Tisdell, *Qualitative Research*.

23. Gadamer, *Truth and Method*.

24. In hermeneutic phenomenology, this is referred to as an "attentive thoughtfulness" and "caring attunement" to the participants. Heidegger, *Being and Time*; van Manen, *Researching Lived Experience*.

# ACKNOWLEDGMENTS

THIS BOOK CAME to fruition over the span of three years from 2020 to 2023. It is not a very long time by book writing measures, but the days, weeks, and months leading up to its completion were among the most intensely difficult and reflective—all at once soul-stirring and soul-fulfilling—in my professional and personal lives to date. Many people, spaces, experiences, and opportunities supported me along the way, knowingly or unknowingly. This will not be a complete list of thanks, but I want to name a few to whom I owe a deep gratitude.

Turina, Lance, Yan, Zong, Mary Ellen, Ben, Colleen, Geraldo, Morna, and many other practitioner colleagues working in or with the community and technical college sector who value, use, and push the research guiding this book;

The National Science Foundation and the Barbara and Glenn Thompson endowed chair I hold, for allowing me to devote time and resources to conduct this research;

Xiwei, Amy, and Peiwen for stellar administrative and research support, and Yen, Ayse, Nicole, and María for thoughtful participation in the larger project;

Connie, Pam, Eboni, Lorenzo, John, Regina, Gloria, Marilyn, Joy, Linda, Lara, Lois, Davis, and countless more professional colleagues whose support and/or scholarship ground my work;

Rachelle, Brian, and all my colleagues in the ELPA department, for the laughter we have shared over the years and continue to share;

My doctoral advisees in the Super Genius group and students in my classes, especially those who traversed the pandemic-impacted educational journey with me over the past four years, for bringing priceless joy and rewards of teaching and mentoring as reflective growth;

Jayne and the Harvard Education Press team who shepherded this book to publication, for your equity-guided vision and steadfast collaboration;

Kelly, for your loving support during times of great difficulty, and for offering an extra set of discerning eyes for data interpretation;

Especially, the 126 educators I interviewed for this book, for your perfectly imperfect efforts to give to your students and colleges, and for endlessly guiding me to new places as a scholar committed to the collective equity agenda of community and technical colleges;

And always, Weijia—my everyday inspiration for all of the things this book is about—for your unconditional support and all the sacrifices you made.

# ABOUT THE AUTHOR

**XUELI WANG** is the Barbara and Glenn Thompson Endowed Professor in Educational Leadership at the University of Wisconsin–Madison. Often centering community and technical colleges, her scholarship spans a range of topics—students' success and mental health, postsecondary trajectories, faculty development, teaching and learning, and educational change and innovation. A notable example of Wang's work is her award-winning book *On My Own: The Challenge and Promise of Building Equitable STEM Transfer Pathways*, published in 2020 by Harvard Education Press. Based on a large-scale longitudinal study, this book unravels enduring inequities in transfer, particularly in science, technology, engineering, and mathematics (STEM) fields of study, and issues a plan of action toward cultivating equitable transfer pathways.

Widely used by researchers and practitioners, Wang's work has been recognized by multiple awards, including the 2021 Publication of the Year award from the American Educational Research Association's Postsecondary Education Division for her book *On My Own*, the Transfer Champion-Catalyst Award by the National Institute for the Study of Transfer Students in 2021, the Barbara Townsend Lecture Award by the Association for the Study of Higher Education in 2020, and the University of Wisconsin–Madison School of Education's Faculty Distinguished Achievement Award in 2020. Wang will serve as president of the Council for the Study of Community Colleges during 2024–2025.

# INDEX